My Journey to Freedom: Kybartai to Haifa

Memoir
by Josef Rosin

Published by JewishGen

An Affiliate of the Museum of Jewish Heritage - A Living Memorial to the Holocaust
New York

My Journey to Freedom: Kybartai to Haifa

Memoir by Josef Rosin

First Printing: October 2013, Tishri 5774
Second Printing: September 2019, Av 5779
Cover Design by Dedi Ben Yehuda and Jan R. Fine
Editor: Nancy Lefkowitz
Layout: Joel Alpert
Publicity: Sandra Hirschhorn

Published by JewishGen, Inc.
An Affiliate of the Museum of Jewish Heritage
A Living Memorial to the Holocaust
36 Battery Place, New York, NY 10280

Printed in the United States of America by Lightning Source, Inc.
Library of Congress Control Number (LCCN): 2013951213
ISBN: 978-1-939561-12-1 (hard cover: 214 pages, alk. paper)

JewishGen and the Yizkor Books in Print Project

This book has been published by the **Yizkor Books in Print Project,** as part of the **Yizkor Book Project** of **JewishGen, Inc**.

JewishGen, Inc. is a non-profit organization founded in 1987 as a resource for Jewish genealogy. Its website [www.jewishgen.org] serves as an international clearinghouse and resource center to assist individuals who are researching the history of their Jewish families and the places where they lived. JewishGen provides databases, facilitates discussion groups, and coordinates projects relating to Jewish genealogy and the history of the Jewish people. In 2003, JewishGen became an affiliate of the **Museum of Jewish Heritage - A Living Memorial to the Holocaust** in New York.

The **JewishGen Yizkor Book Project** was organized to make more widely known the existence of Yizkor (Memorial) Books written by survivors and former residents of various Jewish communities throughout the world. Later, volunteers connected to the different destroyed communities began cooperating to have these books translated from the original language— usually Hebrew or Yiddish—into English, thus enabling a wider audience to have access to the valuable information contained within them. As each chapter of these books was translated, it was posted on the JewishGen website and made available to the general public.

The **Yizkor Books in Print Project** began in 2011 as an initiative to print and publish Yizkor Books that had been fully translated, so that hard copies would be available for purchase by the descendants of these communities and also by scholars, universities, synagogues, libraries, and museums.

These Yizkor books have been produced almost entirely through the volunteer effort of researchers from around the world, assisted by donations from private individuals. The books are printed and sold at near cost, so as to make them as affordable as possible. Our goal is to make this important genre of Jewish literature and history available in English in book form, so that people can have the personal histories of their ancestral towns on their bookshelves for themselves and for their children and grandchildren.

A list of all published translated Yizkor Books can be found at:
http://www.jewishgen.org/Yizkor/ybip.html

Lance Ackerfeld, Yizkor Book Project Manager
Joel Alpert, Yizkor Book in Print Project Coordinator

JewishGen
Yizkor Book Project

This book is presented by the
Yizkor Books in Print Project
Project Coordinator: Joel Alpert

Part of the
Yizkor Books Project of JewishGen, Inc.
Project Manager: Lance Ackerfeld

These books have been produced solely through volunteer effort
of individuals from around the world. The books are printed and
sold at near cost, so as to make them as affordable as possible.

Our goal is to make this history and important genre of Jewish
literature available in English in book form so that people can have
the near-personal histories of their ancestral towns on their bookshelves for themselves and for their children and grandchildren.

Any donations to the Yizkor Books Project are appreciated.

Please send donations to:
Yizkor Book Project
JewishGen
36 Battery Place
New York, NY 10280

JewishGen, Inc. is an affiliate of the
Museum of Jewish Heritage
A Living Memorial to the Holocaust

About the Author, Josef Rosin

A native of Kybartai, Lithuania, Josef Rosin was born on January 24, 1922 to Hayah (nee Leibovitz) from Marijampole, Lithuania and Yehudah Leib Rosin from Sudargas, Lithuania.

He received his elementary and high school education in Kibart, Virbalis and Marijampole. From 1939 he was a student at the Civil Engineering Faculty of the Kovno (Kaunas) University until the war interrupted his studies in June 1941.

Josef lived in the Kovno Ghetto for more than two and a half years until the beginning of February 1944 when he escaped into the woods of Belarus. After the war, in August 1944 he returned to Kovno. At the end of March 1945 Josef left Lithuania and after the tribulations of illegal travel through Poland, Slovakia, Rumania, Hungary, Austria and Italy, he arrived in *Eretz Yisrael* on October 24, 1945 on a ship of *"Ma'apilim" (Illegal Immigrants)*. During the stay in Rumania Josef married Peninah (nee Cypkewitz) from Wloclawek who had made a similarly difficult journey from Poland.

Peninah and Josef on their Wedding Day, Abla Julia, Italy, May 1945

In autumn 1946 Josef started studies at the Civil Engineering Faculty of the Technion. He completed his studies in 1950 earning the degree of Engineer. In 1958 he received the Masters of Science degree in Agricultural Engineering from the Technion. From 1952 until his retirement in 1987 Josef worked at "Water Planning for Israel" (*Tahal*). For more than twenty years he held the position of Head of the Drainage and Development Department of that firm.

Starting after retirement, during the years 1987 through 1994 Josef wrote many entries for the Hebrew book *Encyclopedia of the Jewish Communities in Lithuania (Pinkas Hakehilot-Lita)* acting also as the associate editor; this book, edited by Professor Dov Levin, was published in Hebrew by *Yad Vashem* in 1996.

In 2005 Josef expanded the research he had done for *Pinkas Hakehilot-Lita* and authored the Preserving Our Litvak Heritage - A History of 31 Jewish Communities in Lithuania. In 2006 and 2009 authored two more books, Preserving Our Livak Heritage Volume II and Protecting Our Litvak Heritage, chronicling a total of 102 Lithuanian Jewish towns. These latter books are all in English.

Josef and Peninah have a married son and a married daughter, four grandchildren and two great-granddaughters.

This book is dedicated to the memory of my Father Yehudah-Leib Rosin,

my Mother Khayah nee Leibovitz and my little sister Tekhiyah who were murdered by the Nazis and their Lithuanian helpers.

I thank:

My uncle, the late Dr. Baruh Ben-Jehuda, who helped me find my way through family connections from my mother's side and gave me most of the family's photos.

My cousin, the late Sylvia Rosin-Gendel, who gave me all the pictures of my uncles and their families on my father's side.

My good friend Chaim Galin, who read the manuscript of this book and his important remarks, which were taken into consideration.

My good friend Prof. Dov Levin. Thanks to his encouragement and his useful suggestions I came to publish this book in its present form.

My wife Peninah. Due to her sensitivity regarding human relations, I changed some words and expressions here and there.

My friends Sarah and Mordechai Kopfstein who made my poor English readable.

The daughter of my late cousin Gershon Hilelson, Mrs. Fania Hilelson-Jivotovsky, for helping me to accomplish "The Family Tree" on my father's side.

Finally, I would like to thank all my friends and comrades who helped me to refresh my memory about events that happened 50-60 years ago.

J.R.

Haifa, October 1989 (Updated June 2001)

Remarks on the present edition

This edition is the translation of the Fourth Hebrew Edition issued in September 2000. In this edition I have added many details about my family from my father's side, which I received thanks to the research carried out by my relative and friend Joel Alpert from Boston U.S.A. on the roots of my extended family.

In the text I have marked many names of people mentioned there who have passed away since the previous Hebrew edition of 1992.

In this edition I have also added many photographs of people and objects connected to the events described therein, included several new ones taken in May this year in Lithuania by Nancy Lefkowitz and Marc Shumann in order that my grandchildren and following generations should not have to browse through many albums.

Transliteration of surnames, names of places etc. were done according to the "YIVO" system.

Since the previous English edition issued in 1994, the technical means for printing text and pictures at my disposal have greatly improved, a fact that is certainly obvious in this new edition.

June 2001
J.R.

Meanwhile ten years have passed and we are now in 2011. In this edition I have included a few more family pictures from my mother's side and also added some photos from my own small family. I inserted additional notes here and there and also indicated who among those who I mention in the book have passed away during the past years.

I thank Fania Hilelson-Jivotovsky for editing the added notes.

June 2011
J.R.

Instead of a Foreword

Dear Amikam and Eliyah,

The idea to write my memoirs came into my mind a few years ago, when I recognized that I hadn't told you much about my childhood, about your grandparents, your uncles and cousins, about all the family who were murdered, and about all the hardships and adventures I experienced before I became your father.

I don't want to analyze here the reasons for that. It may be that the reluctance to recall this tragic subject caused me to withhold telling you more about life at home, father and mother, the kind of people they were, and also how your father and mother survived miraculously during these years of horror.

My fate, or may be luck, kept me from witnessing the atrocities which our persecuted nation experienced. Even today, when I read about these atrocities in the many books written by eye witnesses, I am shocked at the cruelty of the murders, and of the thought of how close I was to being involved in a similar situation.

Only after many years did I come to the conclusion that, despite the miracles and the luck I had, day by day and hour by hour, it took a great deal of heroism, then unconscious, to go through all these hardships in order to survive, and also to arrive in Eretz-Yisrael, fulfilling the dream I was brought up to pursue.

I believe that my life story shows, that a nation without its own state lives in a lawless world. If during those years we would have had our own State, many people could have been rescued from the Nazis.

We have to remember that in the thirties, when German Jews were already looking for states of immigration, almost no nation opened its gates to them.

I hope, Ami and Eliyah, that this book, written for you, will allow you to gain deeper insight into the roots of our family, and to comprehend the great loss of growing up without the special grandparents you had.

I also hope that your children, my grandchildren, will in time find interest in this book.

With love,

Father

Table of Contents

Chapter 1: My Hometown Kybartai

The Town and its History

The town Kybartai (Kibart in Yiddish) in Lithuania, where I was born and grew up, is situated on the border of Germany (*East Prussia*). The small stream Liepona, its width was only 4-5 meters, was the border between the empires of Russia and Germany before World War I, and remained the border between Germany and the independent state of Lithuania, which was established after World War I *(See Table 1-The Map of Lithuania)*. Kibart did not exist before the construction of the railway, from St. Petersburg to the German border, in approximately 1865. The site on which Kibart was built was a small village through which the main road to Germany passed. It also served as a station for changing the post horses. The railway station constructed in the village was named Verzhbelova (Virbalis in Lithuanian), after the name of the small town established in the 18th century and situated 4.5 km away from this station's site. During the period of independent Lithuania (1918-1940) and until 1965, the station was called Virbalis. Then the name was changed to Kybartai. During the battle of retreat of the German army in 1944, the luxurious terminal of the station was destroyed.

The size of the station was out of proportion to the size of Kybartai or Virbalis. It consisted of a big terminal with rooms for passengers, for customs, a luxurious restaurant, as well as many tracks and workshops. In one corner of the station there was a long one story building, which, according to rumors, housed the train of the Russian Czars used for their trips abroad. Near the station there was a public garden called the "Railway Garden," with big old trees, paths and benches. In the middle of this garden there was a raised platform with a balcony for an orchestra. At its foot there was a dance floor, which was turned into an ice skating rink in winter. There was also a small building with a primitive bowling alley. Wooden balls of different sizes were used.

Due to the construction of the Russian railway and its connection to the European network, a big part of the Russian import and export trade passed through Kybartai. As a result there was a great need for customs clerks *("Expeditors" as they were called then)*. Many offices were opened in Eydtkuhnen, the small town on the German side of the border, because there were no suitable buildings in Kybartai. Most of the "Expeditors" were Jews who came from the border zones of Russia-Austria and Russia-Germany, and also from Poland. Later on some Jewish "Smugglers" appeared who smuggled immigrants wanting to go to America across the border for payment, who for various reasons did not have a Russian passport. There are some unpleasant stories about this episode.

All of these people, including the railway workers, needed housing, food etc. So after some years, Kibart grew from a tiny village to a small town, increasing in size becoming larger than the older Virbalis. By 1914 Kibart had a population of about 6,000 inhabitants, including about 1,000 Jews, who enjoyed a relatively high standard of living. At the beginning of World War I in August 1914, most of Kibart's Jewish population left the town. Only a few hundred stayed, especially the landlords and house owners. When fighting in the area began, the town changed hands a few times, and a great part of it was destroyed. In the spring of 1915, Kibart was occupied by the German army, who stayed there until the beginning of 1919, when it became a part of independent Lithuania. During the German occupation a part of its former inhabitants returned to Kibart, but because the border no longer existed, there was no longer any need for the customs clerks as well as many other services. As a result, the economic situation deteriorated.

With the establishment of the State of Lithuania, the grand railway station with its warehouses, workshops etc., again became the central customs station for goods from Western Europe into Lithuania and vice versa.

The years between 1919 to 1923 were years of great prosperity for Kibart. All cellars and attics in the town were turned into warehouses. I remember the signs and inscriptions of warehouses left on many buildings in town, but in my time the warehouses did not exist any more. Due to the great shortage of goods, Lithuania was allowed to import almost everything from Germany. Initially, the merchants, mostly Jewish, bought goods in nearby Eydtkuhnen. Later on, they traveled to Berlin with valises and brought back merchandise by themselves. At this time merchants from all over the country started to come to Kibart. The only hotel in town (*it belonged to a Jewish family, Papir*) rented beds by the hour and sometimes people even slept two to a bed.

At that time Kibart had 50 textiles wholesalers, about 10 haberdashery shops, a few leather wholesalers, five private banks, three public banks, and a government bank. The majority of the merchants were Jews. There were also about 50 offices of custom commissioners who employed many people.

The economic prosperity attracted many people to settle in Kibart, including my father and mother.

During these years several modern three-four story buildings were built, like the Shadkhanovitz building, the Seinensky building and others. The Jews established many factories and exported horses and agricultural products.

In a 1922 newspaper article it was reported, that an agent of "Keren Hayesod" *(The Fund of the World Zionist Organization)* named Dr. Vilensky raised $6,000 in one evening from the merchants of Kibart. This newspaper also reported that Kibart Jews acquired stocks of "Bank HaPoalim" (Laborers Bank) that was founded in Eretz-Yisrael at this time.

In 2009 the press published a story stating that owners of stocks of "Jewish Colonial Trust" *(Otsar Hityashvuth HaYehudim-The bank of the Zionist Organization)* or their heirs may claim their value at a special established committee by the Israeli government for this purpose. In the Internet a list of 55,000 stockowners was published. Searching this list I discovered that my father and my uncle Meir purchased three stocks each, two on their names, one on my name (Josef-Dov) and one on the name of my cousin Avraham. The price of each stock was One Pound. I assume that it was in the twenties of the previous century. The stocks were redeemed last year according to the value determined by the government and I got a payment as an heir and as the owner of one stock. In my documents issued in Israel my second name Dov (after my grandfather Dov Rosin who died a short time before my birth) disappeared so I had difficulties proving that I was the owner of the stock. The heirs of Meir and Avraham also received the value of the stocks. *(See the photo of the stock on the name of the known Sarah Aharonson[1] taken by me at the museum "Beit Aharonson" in Zichrom Ya'akov).* It was known in Lithuania, that if funds for Jewish needs was required, that the fundraising would begin in Kovno, the capital, and then proceed to Kibart.

The great prosperity of Kibart ended, when in 1923 Lithuania took over the port town of Klaipeda (Memel) and its zone, situated by the Baltic Sea. The town and the zone belonged to Germany until World War I, after which, according to the Versailles Treaty, it was handed over to the rule of a French High Commissioner. The Lithuanian Government directed a great part of imports and exports, for economic or political reasons, to the port of Memel (Klaipeda in Lithuanian). At the same time the main customs offices were transferred from Kibart

[1] Sarah Aharonson was one of the founders of the Ni'li underground group (abbreviation of *Netsach Israel Lo Iishaker*) whose goal was to help the British army, stationed in Egypt, to free Palestine from the Turkish rule by gathering intelligence on the Turkish army. When the Turkish authorities discovered this group an Turkish officer came to arrest Sarah. She asked for permission to go to the bathroom and there she shot herself with a pistol that was previously hidden there.

to Kovno (Kaunas). As a result, most of the wholesalers and the customs clerks moved to Kovno, and Kibart returned to its pre-boom days. In 1923 the population of Kibart was 6,300 inhabitants, among them 1,253 Jews. Living conditions were quite comfortable.

Photo of the original stock of Sarah Aaronsohn

Life in Kibart was significantly influenced by the closeness of the German border. The main street of the town stretched to the border, which consisted of a wooden bridge over the small stream and customs buildings on either side. These buildings, both on the Lithuanian and German sides of the border, were manned by a policeman and a customs clerk. The inhabitants of a 5 km zone on both sides of the border were issued certificates to enable them to freely cross the border. The town of Eydtkuhnen on the German side of the border was small, but had four-five story buildings, wide paved streets and nice shops, by the standards of the times. Many of the merchants, who owned textile, shoe, clothes and other stores, were Jews. Eydtkuhnen also had "White Weeks" and "Seasonal Sales."

The Border Crossing between Kibart and Eydtkuhnen

Until 1933, the beginning of the Nazi regime, we bought most of our supplies in Eydtkuhnen, including fruits which we could not obtain in Kibart, such as bananas, grapes, watermelons, melons etc., and for reasonable prices. Before "Pesakh" Mother prepared a stock of oranges and tangerines at home. The problem was how to cross the border without paying customs fees. The method was to take only two-three oranges in a paper bag by hand when crossing the border. New shoes were smeared with shoe polish and not brushed, so they did not look new to the custom's clerk.

The German inhabitants of the border zone crowded the market of Kibart to stock up on fresh agricultural products, which were plentiful in Lithuania and cheaper than in Germany.

There were times, during the late twenties, when my parents went to the cinema in Eydtkuhnen. Once they even went to a circus show in Stalupoenen, some 20 km from the border.

In 1933, when the Nazis came to power, all this stopped. I remember on April 1, 1933 when I went with my mother to Eydtkuhnen and guards of the S.A. Nazis didn't allow us into Jewish stores. From that day on we stopped going to Eydtkuhnen.

Lithuania's main export items were agricultural products, most of them going to Germany. One of the major products exported to Germany was live geese. At the beginning of winter, the exporters would bring the geese to a lot in the railway station, not far from our apartment. We heard the quacking of the geese day and night for a month or so. When Hitler's rule in Germany was stabilized, he demanded Memel's return to Germany. As a means of pressure he cancelled the commercial treaty with Lithuania, so all the geese assigned for export were left without buyers. To solve the problem, the Lithuanian government ordered that all its clerks would get a part of their salary in geese. During those days the price of geese dropped a lot. I remember the taste of roasted geese and the schmaltz that Mother prepared at home.

The railway station in Kibart reminds me of more events. All the immigrants *(Olim)* to Eretz-Yisrael traveled by train through this station. There were years, when every few weeks a group of "Khalutzim" *(members of "HeChalutz"-Pioneer organization)* went through Kibart. Large crowds of Jews came to see them off. These were happy and exciting events, sometimes even funny. In order to exploit every "Certificate" *(Aliyah Permission),* issued by the British Mandatory Government, to its maximum, every young man married a girl fictitiously, so that each "Certificate" enabled two people to enter Eretz-Yisrael. It happened many times that the fictitious couple met for the first time in the station in Kibart, and the "groom" looked for the "bride" he had never met by shouting her name.

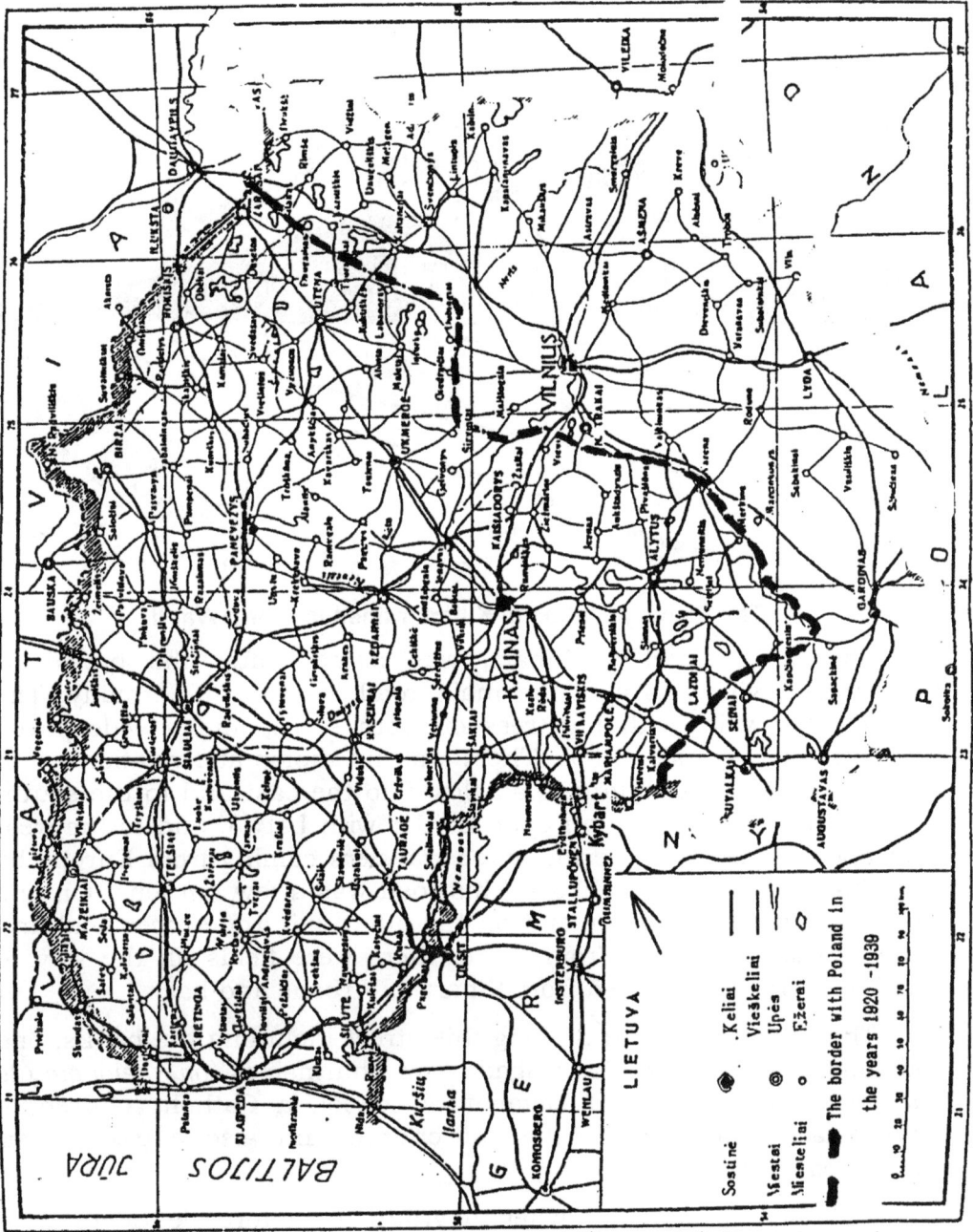

Map of Lithuania

The Railway Station in Kibart, ruined in World War II

The main street of Kibart, was named after the president, Smetona Blvd., was also the main road leading to Germany. The street was wide, with big trees on both sides, and a wide paved sidewalk on one side of it. There was no diplomatic relations with Poland therefore Lithuania was closed to the east and to the south. To the north there was an open border with Latvia, and to the west an open border with Germany, so travelers coming from Europe by car had to go through Kibart. This road was a few km long. On one side of it was the border and on the other side the soccer field and the Jewish cemetery. From there, there were fields all the way to Virbalis. We often walked from Kibart to Virbalis and back.

The stores were found along this street including the banks, one cinema, the volunteer fire brigade, two pharmacies (*one belonging to a Jew*), the government elementary school, a Catholic church, a Pravoslavic church, a Protestant church and also a gas station operated by hand.

I recall one occasion when a group of motorcycle riders from "Hapoel" Eretz-Yisrael passed Kibart. They bought gas at this station. This was a big event in Kibart.

The House and the Apartment

The house we lived in was situated on the main street, Smetona Blvd. 63, and was built in 1920. Except for central heating, the house had all the usual conveniences. It was a three-story building with an attic and a cellar. The cellar served as cold storage for some foods, instead of a refrigerator not common in those days. We also stored in it heating materials like wood, coal and peat. There was also a well in the cellar. By rotating a vertical wheel, the attendant of the house pumped water from the well through a pipe to a concrete reservoir in the attic. From that reservoir all flats received their water. Some years before the war we received the water from the municipal water supply. The sewage outlet of the house was an absorbent pit, as there was no central sewage system in the town. We received electricity from the power station which was owned by the railway. I have to point out, that in the twenties there were many small towns in Lithuania without electricity and certainly no sewage or bathrooms in the houses. In the village of Sudarg, where my Father's married sister lived with many children and where we went for summer vacation, I met a boy of 15, who had never seen electric light in his life, since all the lighting there was by kerosene lamps. At my grandparents' in Mariampol the toilet was in a small hut in the back yard, but electricity was there ever since I can remember.

The house we lived in was situated on the corner of two streets. On the side facing the main street, there were three shops on the first floor, one of them used by the house's landlord (Shadkhanovitz), the two others were rented. On the other side of the street there were two shops; one of them was at one time our shop. On the two upper floors there were four flats, two on each floor. From the main entrance to the house we would go through the stairwell into the backyard. It was a big square plot, surrounded on three sides by buildings and on the fourth side by a high wooden fence. This fence had a wicket and a gate. One of the buildings served as the stockroom for our shop and that of the house owner. At one corner of the backyard there was an underground concrete reservoir for garbage, which was emptied from time to time by a special contractor. In the middle of the plot there was a well operated by a hand pump. The entrance to the basement flat of the housekeeper and his family was from the backyard. The entrance doors to the house were locked at night and every tenant had a key to the main door.

Our flat was on the third floor of the house. Above it was an attic that was covered by a sloping tiled roof. We had four rooms; the entrance to them was through a corridor. There were also doors from one room to another. All rooms were on one side of the flat in the direction of the main street. At the edge of the corridor there was the bathroom, next to it the kitchen and in it the entrance to the toilet. These rooms were on the side of the backyard.

When I was a little boy there was no bathroom in our flat. The bath was installed only during the thirties. Before this, we washed in the kitchen in a big tin bathtub. In the kitchen there was a big stove built of bricks surfaced with white tiles. The heating materials were wood and coal and later also peat. For small meals we used a primus.

The Occupations of the Jews in Kibart

During those times the main occupation of the Jews was in commerce. There were a variety of shops selling items including: haberdashery, groceries, shoes, cloth, paper, books, stationary, meat, iron, tools, and household utensils. There were also several small factories engaged in bookbinding, also a shoe polish and tin cans factory, several textile factories, and sewing workshops etc. There were many craftsmen: shoemakers, photographers, tailors, dressmakers, barbers etc. Some people were exporters of agricultural products, such as flax, after it was processed in town, as well as horses for meat. Apart from those there was one cinema owner, two tavern owners, several custom clerks, teachers, bank clerks, two carriages and one taxi owner. The economic life in town centered on the Jewish Central Bank and the Jewish Popular Bank. There were two especially Jewish occupations in town: one illegal, trade with foreign currency and the other, "Couriers." These were people who traveled every morning by train to Kovno and returned in the evening. They passed on orders from the merchants of Kibart to the wholesalers in Kovno, and then brought the ordered goods back on the same day by themselves. They also sold smuggled merchandise from Germany to the rich merchants in Kovno. There were seven families who did not do well in this job and they barely earned a living. I remember at least one case when the community had to buy the monthly train ticket for one of those couriers, because the man did not have the money for it.

The Public and Cultural Life

As I mentioned before, most of the Jews settled in Kibart after World War I, so they didn't know each other previously. This was due to the fact that everybody was called by his family name, and not, as was common in the old Jewish villages, where everyone had a nickname according to the village his grandfather came from, or related to his occupation, or to the name of his mother or grandmother. My grandfather, who lived in Mariampol, was called

"Jankel the Shokhet" *(Slaughterer)* and not Jankel Leibovitz, which was his family name. In Israel I met people born in Mariampol, who knew my mother only as "The daughter of Jankel the Shokhet."

In the twenties, Kibart established the Hebrew elementary six-grade school, two synagogues, a bathhouse, a "Mikveh," and a lending library with many books in Hebrew and Yiddish. It was there that I began to borrow books in both languages as a young boy.

Help organizations for the poor and the needy, such as "Ezrah" and "Linath Hatsedek," were established, as well as the "OZE" organization, which provided a glass of milk for poor children and also financed their stay at summer camps. Sometimes a drama circle acted in Kibart, performing different plays.

The great synagogue was built of red bricks and was located opposite the market square. The synagogue was a big two story building, with the "Ezrath Nashim" *(Women's Gallery)* on the second floor. In addition to the prayer hall, which included the "Bimah" *(Podium)* and the beautiful "Aron Kodesh" *(The Holy Ark),* there were other rooms, serving different purposes. The synagogue, the bathhouse, the "Mikveh" and the library were all on one block.

The small synagogue "Ohel-Yitskhak" was at the other end of town. My uncle Meir was their "Ba'al Kore" *(The reader of the "Torah" with the proper tune).* He fulfilled this duty until his death. His firstborn son Avraham (died in Tel Aviv) and his firstborn grandson Meir (lived with his family in Tel Aviv) also learned to read the "Torah." (Avraham and his son Meir are not with us any longer).

The synagogue still stands but is used for other purposes.

Chapter 2: The Family

On Mother's side

My mother's parents were Yakov Leibovitz and Zisle nee Telshitz *(See the Family Tree up to the grandchildren of my cousins-Tables 3).* Grandma Zisle's father was also Yakov. In his old age he lived with his wife Peshe in Mariampol. He was a "Shokhet" and a Cantor and passed on his profession to his son-in-law. The Telshitz family included, in addition to Grandma Zisle, two more sisters, Khayah and Taube, and one son Joseph (Josl). Khayah and Taube immigrated to America, married and had families. The family name of Khayah was Copland and that of Taube, Gold (short for Goldberg). The sons of Josl, Yehudah, Shemuel-David and Anshel (Hans) also immigrated to America, where they changed their family name to Telser. While I was writing this book, Anshel was still living in Chicago. The son of Shemuel-David, Eugene, who lives in San Diego, California, is working at this time (2001) to put together a detailed family tree. *(Passed away recently)*

Ya'akov and Peshe Telshitz

Josl also had two daughters. One was Esther Gidansky, who lived in Memel, until the Nazis took over the town. Then she moved to Kovno and was later imprisoned in the Kovno Ghetto. After the liquidation of the Ghetto, she was transferred to the concentration camp Stutthof in Germany and it was there that she perished. Her son Yakov lives in Tel Aviv, and her daughter Paula, in America. Yakov is married and has one daughter, Ophirah, who is a graphic artist. Paula is widowed. She has one son Ariel Stone, who lives in Paris. The second daughter of Josl was Perl Kubovitsky, who emigrated in the fifties with her husband Yitskhak from Belgium to Israel and died in Israel a few years ago. They had two daughters, Lizet *(Ahuva)* and Simon *(Shimona)*, and one son, Shaul. Lizet disappeared during World War II, while trying to escape with her brother from the Nazis in occupied Belgium to Switzerland. Simon lived in America and had one daughter, Jacqueline Abramov. Shaul lives in Jerusalem. He is married and before retiring was a judge specializing in labor issues. He has two daughters, Daphnah and Anath.

Grandpa Yakov came from Kelm (Kelme) a small town north of Kovno, famous for its "Yeshivah." His father was Meir Leibovitz Braude, *(Leibovitz-meaning son of Leib, as was customary in Russia).* At the time, 'only' sons in the family were not drafted into the Czars' army. In order to avoid the draft, Yakov dropped the Braude from his family name, it became Leibovitz and thus he was an 'only' son. The other brothers remained Braude. Yakov had three brothers and one sister: Yisrael Braude, who immigrated to South Africa (Capetown?); Aharon, who immigrated to America, where he changed his name to Brody; Barukh, who died young in Kovno. My uncle Barukh was named after him. His sister Rachel married a relative Braude and lived in Leipzig-Germany.

When I was a little boy, my mother, my sister and I went to Mariampol every summer to visit our grandparents. They lived in a small two family wooden house on one of the main streets of the town, Pren Street.

Grandpa, as I remember him, was short, lean and had a graybeard. He wore a traditional long coat *(Capota)* and was a "Mithnaged" *(Opponent of the "Chasidim"),* as most Lithuanian Jews were. He made his living as a "Shokhet." Despite being a little boy, I remember hearing about the endless trouble my Grandpa had because of the rivalry of another "Shokhet" in town. When he became ill, Mother brought Grandpa and Grandma to live with us. After a short illness he died at the age of 70 in 1932. He was buried in the Jewish cemetery in Kibart. On his grave, a special tombstone called a "Ohel" was built. It was a little house built of red bricks with a sloping roof and with a marble plaque in front. The inscription on it was written by uncle Barukh, who sent it from Tel Aviv *(See photo)* On a photo of that cemetery which was taken by a Jew at the beginning of the 1970's, the "Ohel" was still standing. Grandma Zisle and Uncle Meir were also buried in this cemetery.

In May of this year (2001) a group of relatives from America, headed by Joel Alpert and Fania Hilelson-Jivotovsky, visited the Kibart cemetery and took pictures of the still existing headstones there. Grandpa's "Ohel" is partly ruined, but the headstone exists *(see photo)*.

Grandma Zisle gave birth to seven children, four of them died in childhood of diphtheria. The youngest was Benjamin, who died at the age of four and I remember Grandma mourning him. Her three children who survived to adulthood were Uncle Meir, my mother Khayah and Uncle Barukh. The latter immigrated to Eretz-Yisrael in 1911 at the age of 17, and changed his family name to Ben-Yehudah. Grandma was short and roundish, and wore a brown wig. She was not well educated by today's standards, but could read and write in Yiddish and also read the prayers in Hebrew. Plate 7 in the Appendix shows an example of the many letters she wrote to Avraham in Yiddish. She had a few books in Yiddish, which were common for Jewish women, with simple commentaries of the Bible.

After Grandpa's death, Grandma moved from Mariampol to live with us. My parents gave her a room in our apartment, where she lived. In it there was a bookcase with religious books, which had belonged to her husband. Among these books were the "Talmud-Bavli" bound with leather from the famous Publishing House, "The Widow and Brothers Rom" from Vilna and the "Talmud-Yerushalmi." There was also the complete "Shulkhan-Arukh" *(Code of Jewish Laws and Customs)*, as well as many other books and booklets, among them the booklets that Grandpa wrote himself: "Khemdath Ya'akov," Warsaw 1901 and "Meir Ikvei Ish," Grajewe 1911. I prepared a catalogue of all these books, which, to my great regret, was lost in the Holocaust.

During the time that Grandma was healthy, she actively participated in everything with us, but the antagonism between her generation and that of Mother's was tremendous, causing occasional quarrels between them. In her last years she got wounds on the lower part of her feet. All the ointments the doctors prescribed didn't help. She died in our apartment on March 13, 1940.

Uncle Meir was a few years older then my mother. In his youth he studied in a "Yeshiva," as was customary in those times. He married a beautiful woman (nee Frank), who gave birth to Meir's firstborn son, Avraham. She died of tuberculosis after they were married a few years. Some years later Meir married Sarah Prakherkrug from Virbalis. They had two sons Aryeh (Leib) and Elyakim, and a girl Tsiporah (Malka'le). Aryeh was one year younger than me.

Meir died from esophageal cancer at the Government Hospital in Kovno in 1940 and was buried in the Jewish cemetery in Kibart. His wife and children were murdered by the Nazis in July, 1941.

As said before, Aunt Zisle and Uncle Meir were buried in the Jewish cemetery in Kibart. Both died during the Soviet rule and I doubt if headstones were placed at their graves. The pictures of the headstones taken by Nancy Lefkowitz at the cemetery in 2001, do not include Zisle's or Meir's.

ספר

חמדת יעקב

בו יבאר כל התעליות פרוח ודקית היוצאת מחמשת חומשי תורה ומנביאים

ראשונים לקומות בקצרה מס' ולב"ג

מאתי המחבר

יעקב לייבאוויץ שי"ב

בלא"א הר"ר מאיר ברודא

יליד קעלץ

תהן רמה מא"יאספאל

וואַרשא

כדפום הגבערוש מרט נאלעווקי 39

שנת "כום יך טוב טעני ברמט" לפ"ק

СЕФЕРЪ

ХЕМДАОъ ЯКОВъ

т. е. Охота Израила

соч. Я. ЛЕЙВОВИЧъ

ВАРШАВА

въ Тип. Б. Туршъ, Варшава. Налевки № 39.

The front page of Josef's maternal grandfather's book "Khemdath Ya'akov"
Published in Warsaw in 1901

1933

2001 *(Photo taken by Marc Schumann)*

Tomb and tombstone of Grandpa Yakov at the Jewish cemetery in Kibart

Grandma near our shop

Grandma Zisle in her elderly days reading a religious book in our kitchen ("Tsena U'rena")

Initially Meir was my father's partner in a paper and stationary store. This was located in the same building we lived in, however not on its front side but around the corner, on a perpendicular street. Meir and his family lived in the same building, which belonged to Shadkhanovitz. After several years disputes arose between the partners, and the partnership broke up. As far as I understood at that time, I was a little boy then Meir didn't know how to handle money and was probably a bad tradesman. He was a communal worker, made speeches on every occasion, he liked to sing and, as mentioned before, was the "Ba'al-Kore" *(Torah Reader)* in the little synagogue until he became ill. For many years Meir was the chairman of the parents' committee of the elementary Hebrew School. His picture appears on many graduation class photos of this school.

After the partnership with my father ended, Meir opened a stationary and bookshop, also on the main street opposite the Pravoslav church. His family left the apartment in the Shadkhanovitz building and moved to a cheaper one, not far from the great synagogue, which belonged to a Lithuanian house owner. Meir also opened a small workshop for cardboard boxes and, if I am not mistaken, also a bookbindery. After some time he ended up in debt and his employees expropriated the workshop in lieu of the salaries he owed them.

Meir's firstborn son from his first wife, Avraham, was not happy at home for different reasons. My mother supported him spiritually and sometimes gave him pocket money. In 1934, when uncle Barukh visited us in Kibart, he convinced Meir to send Avraham to Eretz-Yisrael, and in 1935 he indeed moved there. He studied at the "Herzeliyah" high school in Tel Aviv and later at the Hebrew University Law School in Jerusalem. He married Shulamith (nee Federman). They had two sons: Meir and David, also three daughters: Rachel, Tsiporah and Khanah. All are married and have children. Avraham and Shulamith have already passed away.

Meir's second son, Aryeh (Leibke), was active in the Zionist Youth Organization of "HaShomer HaTsair." He wore shorts most of the year and spoke mainly Hebrew. He graduated the Hebrew High School in Mariampol in 1940, when Lithuania was already a Soviet Republic. This was in fact the last graduating class of that school. Elyakim went to elementary school with my sister Tekhiyah. They both appear on the graduation class photo of 1938. I don't remember much about Tsiporah.

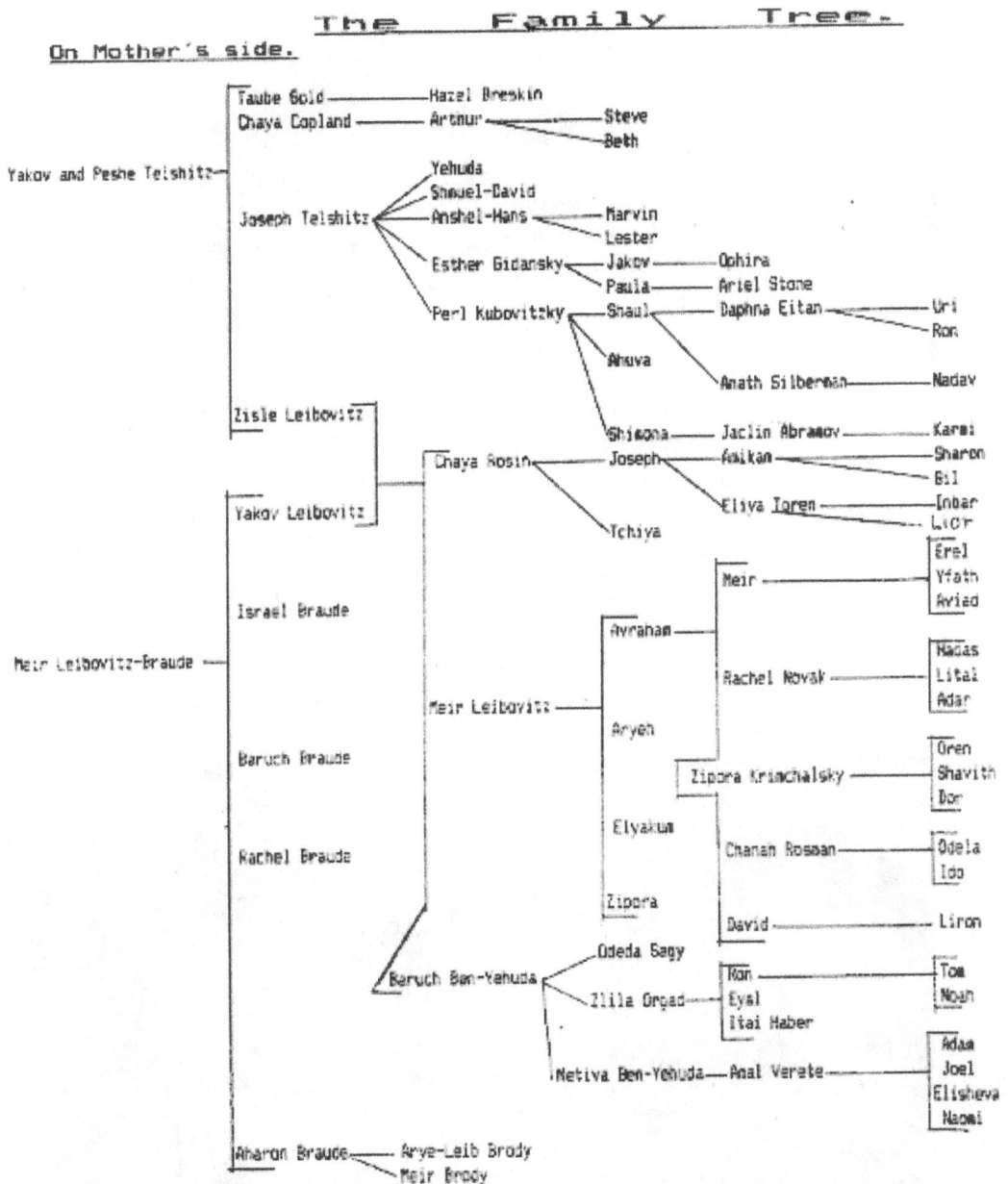

The Family Tree Mother's side

Table 3

The Family Tree.
On Mother's side.

```
Yakov and Peshe Telshitz─┐
                         │   Taube Gold──────Hazel Breskin
                         │   Chaya Copland──────Arthur──────Steve
                         │                              └──Beth
                         │                    Yehuda
                         │                    Shmuel-David
                         │   Joseph Telshitz──Anshel-Hans──────Marvin
                         │                              └──Lester
                         │            Esther Bidansky──Jakov──────Ophira
                         │                         └─Paula──────Ariel Stone
                         │            Perl Kubovitzky──Shaul──────Daphna Eitan──────Uri
                         │                                                       └─Ron
                         │                         Ahuva
                         │                              Anath Silberman──────Nadav
         Zisle Leibovitz─┤
                         │                         Shimona──────Jaclin Abramov──────Karmi
                         │   Chaya Rosin──────Joseph──────Amikan──────Sharon
                         │                                                  └─Gil
                         │                              Eliya Toren──────Inbar
         Yakov Leibovitz─┘                         Tchiya                 └─Lior
                                                                       Erel
                                                          Meir──────Yfath
                                                                    Aviad
         Israel Braude           Avraham                          Hadas
                                                 Rachel Novak──────Lital
                                                                   Adar
Meir Leibovitz-Braude─┐   Meir Leibovitz──┐
                      │                    Aryeh                 Oren
                      │                        Zipora Krimchalsky──────Shavith
         Baruch Braude│                                               Dor
                      │                    Elyakum
                      │                        Chanan Rosman──────Odela
         Rachel Braude│                                          Ido
                      │                    Zipora
                      │                        David──────Liron
                      │             Odeda Sagy
                      │   Baruch Ben-Yehuda──┐           Ron──────Tom
                      │                   Zlila Orgad──Eyal       Noah
                      │                              Itai Haber
                      │                                            Adam
                      │   Netiva Ben-Yehuda──Anal Verete──────Joel
                      │                                           Elisheva
                      │                                           Naomi
         Aharon Braude──────Arye-Leib Brody
                      └──Meir Brody
```

Uncle Meir with his second wife Sarah
and the two children Avraham and Aryeh 1924

Avraham and me before his Aliyah
1934

My cousin Odedah (Dedi) Ben
Yehuda

The visit of uncle Barukh in Mariampol in 1923
Standing from right: Father, Yafa-Barukh's wife,
Odeda, Barukh, Meir.
Sitting from right: Mother and on her knees I the baby,
Grandma and Grandpa, Sarah-Meir's wife
and at her feet Avraham.

Meir, Ima, Barukh, 1934

The visit of Uncle Barukh in Kibart in 1934
Standing from right: I and my cousins Avraham and Aryeh.
Sitting from right: Father, Mother, Barukh, Grandma, Meir, Sarah.
Sitting on the lower line: Tkhiya, Tsipora, Elyakim.

Uncle Barukh was born in Mariampol in 1894 and was the youngest of my grandparents' three children. At the age of three he could read already, and at the age of seven was acquainted with the Pentateuch. At fifteen he studied "Talmud" by himself. In short, he was an "Ilui" (*Genius*). After he read some books, specifically the book of A.Mapu "Ahavath Zion," *(Love of Zion)* and listened to a speech of an emissary from Eretz-Yisrael, he decided at the age of sixteen and a half to emigrate to Eretz-Yisrael.

His father did not even want to hear about it, but Barukh did not give up. He saved money by giving Hebrew grammar and Bible lessons. At the age of 16.5 years he already had the necessary money for the trip. Being a minor, he needed his father's signature on the passport application form, but his father refused to sign. Only after many attempts of persuasion from his mother and sister, did he get his father's signature, and left for the Promised Land. For more than two years his father did not write to him or read his letters. They reconciled only when Barukh came for a visit to Mariampol.

From left: Dov Levin, Netivah Ben Yehudah, Josef and Peninah

**From right: Ami, Peninah, Amal (Netivah's only daughter),
her husband Yoram Verete at their house in Kelil, 1995**

He graduated "Herzeliyah" high school. During World War I, when citizens of Tel Aviv were deported by the Turks, he was a Hebrew teacher in Kibbutz Degania A'. In 1920 he went to Brussels University, having received a grant from a fund established by Baron Rothschild. There he received his Ph.D. degree in Physics and Mathematics, with highest distinction. Before going to Brussels he married Yafa (nee Turkenitz), whose father was one of the first Hebrew teachers in Eretz-Yisrael, and lived most of his years in Rosh Pina. In Brussels their first daughter Odeda (Dedi) was born.

After returning to Tel Aviv, Barukh began his long career (42 years) as a teacher, educator and director of the "Herzeliyah" school. Before the establishment of the State of Israel, Barukh was the director of the Education Department of the "Va'ad Leumi" *(National Committee)* and later the first General Director of the Ministry for Education and Culture of the State of Israel. He published many textbooks on Mathematics, Zionism, the Hebrew calendar, Education, "Ta'amei HaMikra"*(Special musical notes for chanting the*

Torah) etc, also a story, entitled "All are Loved." He also published many articles on different subjects.

He was the founder of the youth organization "Makhanoth HaOlim," whose members were among the founders of the Kibutzim "Maoz Khayim" and "Beth HaShitah." He also lectured at the Hebrew University in Jerusalem on the Methodic of Mathematics.

His eldest daughter Odedah (Dedi) is a graphic artist, married, no children; the second, Tslilah (Lili), is an art critic and has three sons.

The youngest daughter Netivah (Tiva) has one daughter (Amal). Tiva was a sabotage officer in the "Palmach" Brigade during Israel's War of Independence and wrote two books about this period. She also published, together with Dan Ben-Amotz, two volumes of "The Dictionary of Spoken Hebrew."

In 1981 "The Book of Dr. Barukh Ben-Yehudah" was published in his honor by a public committee. A family tree in this book shows, that the roots of the Braude-Leibovitz family trace back to the famous Rabbi "Maharal" of Prag *(Yehuda Liva ben Betsalel 1512-1609). (See Table 2)*

The tombstone on the grave of Rabbi Yehudah ben Betsalel Liva (Maharal) at the old Jewish cemetery in Prague.

(Picture by Josef's daughter Elia February 10, 2010)

Mother, whose name was Khayah, was born in 1888 in Mariampol. In her youth she was a very pretty girl, with blond hair and green eyes. Many young men courted her. The most serious one was her cousin Yehudah Telshitz. The young couple was planning to marry, but their parents objected, because of the fear of marriage among relatives. Yehudah later immigrated to America. Finally she married my father on July 31, 1920. The matchmaker was Shaul Rogalsky from Sudarg, the village my father lived in and who had relatives in Mariampol. (His two daughters are: Sarah, who lives in Israel, and the late Batyah Coblentz in Johannesburg, both have passed away).

Father inherited a house from his parents, also a small shop in Sudarg. He traded flax. After the wedding, the young couple lived in Sudarg for some time. Later on they moved to Kibart, where they rented the apartment in the Shadkhanovitz building, which had been recently built. It was in this building that Father and Uncle Meir opened the stationary store. My sister and I were born in this apartment. From this apartment Father was taken out to his murder, and a few weeks later also mother and sister. The building was destroyed during the battles for the reoccupation of Kibart by the Red Army in World War II.

I don't know how Mother learned everything she knew. She didn't study in a Russian high school, but she could read and write well in Hebrew, Yiddish, German, Russian and a little Lithuanian. In our flat there were books in all those languages. The daily newspaper we read was in Yiddish.

Khayah, Barukh and Meir Leibovitz at the beginning of the century

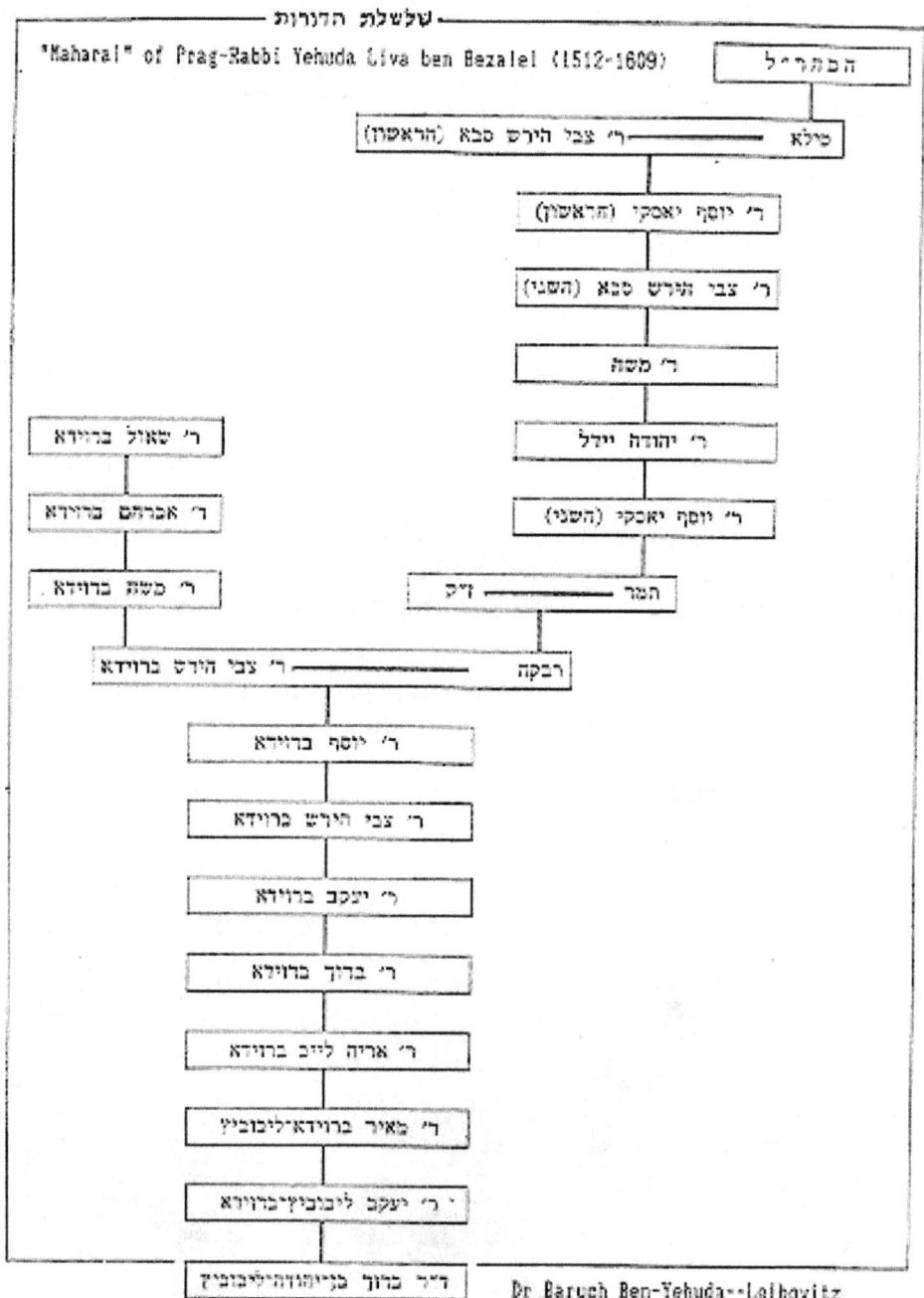

Table 2

———— שלשלת הדורות ————

| "Maharal" of Prag-Rabbi Yehuda Liva ben Bezalel (1512-1609) | המהר״ל |

מילא ——————— ר׳ צבי הירש סבא (הראשון)

ר׳ יוסף יאסקי (הראשון)

ר׳ צבי הירש סבא (השני)

ר׳ משה

ר׳ יהודה יידל

| ר׳ שאול ברוידא | | ר׳ יוסף יאסקי (השני) |

| ר׳ אברהם ברוידא | | התמר ——— זיק |

| ר׳ משה ברוידא | |

ר׳ צבי הירש ברוידא ——————— רבקה

ר׳ יוסף ברוידא

ר׳ צבי הירש ברוידא

ר׳ יעקב ברוידא

ר׳ ברוך ברוידא

ר׳ אריה לייב ברוידא

ר׳ מאיר ברוידא-ליבוביץ

ר׳ יעקב ליבוביץ-ברוידא

| ד״ר ברוך בן-יהודה-ליבוביץ | Dr Baruch Ben-Yehuda--Leibovitz |

Mother as a young woman

Father and Mother-Khayah and Yehudah-Leib Rosin at their wedding, 1920

The wedding picture of Father and Mother, Kovno 1921

Standing from right: Khayah Hilelson, Father and Mother, Meir Leibovitz and Khanah Saalkind.

Sitting from right: Grandpa Ber-Dov Rosin, Grandma Zisle and Grandpa Yakov Leibovitz

Josef at the age of 4-5

Tekhiyah and Josef at a visit in Mariampol

Tekhiyah with her cousin Tsiporah, about 1933   Tekhiyah in 1939-40

I have letters written by Mother, in German, during the years 1915-1917, to her brother Barukh, who lived then in Deganiah A'. During the years of World War I, Lithuania was under German occupation. In the letters presented in Tables 4 & 4a there are regards written by Grandma in Gothic type letters, by Grandpa in Latin letters, and by Meir in Gothic letters. My parents had many German friends in Kibart and in Eydtkuhnen, and Mother spoke with them in fluent German. Several Russian citizens, who lived in Kibart were happy to speak with Mother in their mother tongue. In 1940, when an officer of the Soviet Border Guard was lived in our apartment, I often heard Mother speak fluent Russian with him.

I have in my possession many letters written by Mother in Hebrew to her brother Barukh in Tel Aviv. (see table 5 that shows a photocopy of a letter written by Mother in 1935, when our family was planning to immigrate to Eretz -Yisrael.)

Mother had a good musical ear and a nice voice. She liked to sing songs in Yiddish, Hebrew, as well as sing cantoral music. She had a violin, which she played by ear as well as from written music. Classical music was unknown in the house of the "Shokhet" of Mariampol. Mother was also very good in handicrafts. I remember the birds she made from empty eggshells to decorate the apartment for "Shavuoth." She also made toys from plywood, the figures drawn by scorching it with a special instrument. My cousin Lili has a plywood jewelry box my Mother made and she gave it to her brother Barukh as a present. In our apartment we had embroidery and knitting items Mother made in her youth.

Politically, mother was a Socialist-Zionist and for many years we were subscribers to the Jewish daily newspaper "Dos-Vort" (The Letter), published by the Zionist-Socialist organization. Mother was the chairwoman of "WIZO" (Women International Zionist Organization) chapter in Kibart and arranged different activities for its members. I helped my mother by painting big placards for these activities in Yiddish, and by attaching them to the window of the Jewish pharmacy of Tilzer & Gershater. I remember the farewell party the women of "WIZO" arranged in our apartment for Mrs. Vizhansky and Mrs. Shatenshtein before they left with their families to Eretz-Yisrael. (see photo). I also remember the "Bazaar" of "WIZO" which took place in Kibart where jewelry produced by "Betsalel" from Eretz-Yisrael was sold. The festive opening of the "Bazaar" took place in the hall of the local cinema. Mother opened the festivities by standing on the stage where she and others gave short welcome speeches. She wore a black silk gown and looked very elegant. I remember mother's excitement because she had to deliver a speech before a big audience. She was not a speechmaker like Uncle Meir, who was able to give a speech for every occasion. Sometimes it was difficult for him to end his speech!

Mother, like many Jewish mothers, was anxious, but she didn't restrict me too much. Nevertheless, sometimes I had to argue a little with her.

She allowed me to bathe in the small stream, which was the border between Lithuania and Germany. To go there we needed a police permit, for which we paid a small fee. I was then a little boy and I didn't know how to swim. There was no lifeguard.

There were things Mother wanted me to do or learn, and there were things I wanted to have. Usually most of those things came true. Mother wanted me to learn to play a violin. At the age of 10 or 11, my parents bought me a violin. I took lessons from an elderly German, who played the organ in the Protestant Church in Kibart. After one or two years, I moved to a Lithuanian teacher, a graduate of the conservatory in Memel (Klaipeda). I studied with him until I moved to high school in Mariampol. There I played once with a band at a school Hanukah dance. After that I stopped playing.

Before my Bar Mitzvah, my parents, especially mother, wanted me to learn a little Talmud. They did not have high expectations, but they wanted me to know at least something about it. They found a man from somewhere, who lived on a bench in the Synagogue. I studied with him during the summer of 1934 a few tractates of the Talmud (Baba Bathra).

In the summer of 1936 the youth organization "HaShomer-HaTsair" in Lithuania organized the "Shomriyah." This was a meeting of all members of the movement, which took place in a forest on the bank of the river Neman, (Nemunas) not far from Kovno. The meeting lasted for several days. The participants stayed overnight in a big tent camp there. It was obvious that not all members of the movement attended the meeting. Some could not afford the cost of travel and participation fees. Not all parents allowed their young children to travel alone from all over Lithuania to Kovno.

I was 14 years old and my parents allowed me to attend. I traveled by train to Kovno with a few friends and from there we went by organized transportation to the "Shomriyah."

It was a great and exciting event. Several memories have stayed with me all these years. The meeting with Jewish youth from many towns, whose names I had never heard before, was an exciting experience. Also the meeting with the leadership of the movement, every one of them dressed in a Scout uniform, made a significant impression on me. One of the leaders who impressed me very much was Eliyahu Beilis. Later on he became the Director of a well-known school of the Labor trend in North Tel Aviv. Years later I met him in Tel Aviv. I had found out that his school was growing vegetables on the lot that my father had bought some years ago. The lot was opposite the school, and when I asked Mr. Beilis to clear it, because I wanted to sell it, he did so very quickly.

When I was at the "Shomriya" I read in a newspaper, that General Franco had started a war against the Republican Government of Spain. Then, of course, I could not appreciate the significance of this event, which in fact was the overture to World War II with all its atrocities.

At that time my parents bought me a used ladies bicycle. The idea was that Mother would also learn how to ride. I, of course, learned quickly, but Mother soon gave up the idea, after she had fallen once, injured her knees and tore her socks. This bicycle broke down very often, so we sold it back to the locksmith from whom we had bought it. In the autumn of 1939 refugees from Poland arrived in Lithuania. Among them were soldiers who escaped from the defeated Polish Army. One of them rode a military bicycle with wider then usual tires. We bought that bicycle from him, but I enjoyed it for only one year.

In the summer of 1939, after graduating from high school, my comrades David Shadkhanovitz and Khanan Helperin and me decided to go by bicycle to the farm of our mutual friend Mosheh Vald. The trip was expected to take two or three days in one direction, staying overnight with relatives. David's mother did not let him go. Khanan and I went to the farm and returned safely. Many years after I came to Israel, I received the photo that was taken on this farm, from Moshe's cousin, who was also there and appears in that photo. Khanan Helperin was shot on the first day of the war, when the German Army entered Kibart. Mosheh Vald, his parents and his sister were murdered a month later.

In the summer of 1940, after the annexation of Lithuania to the Soviet Union, the government started an "Agrarian Reform," the purpose of which was to divide the land of the big estates into small plots, and to hand these over to the peasants. The relevant office borrowed my bicycle for the use of an assistant surveyor. This man broke my bicycle and was obliged to pay me back its price, but in this summer my parents bought me a new bicycle made by "Opel" of Germany. I took it with me to Kovno where I rode it to the University.

The old part of Kovno was built in the valley, where the river Viliya *(Neris in Lithuanian)* joins the river Neman *(Nemunas).* Through the ages, the city had grown and spread out over the hills surrounding this valley. I lived on a hill called "The Green Hill." The University was on another hill on the opposite side of the Neman, called Alexot (Aleksotas). I arrived at the University by riding my bicycle downhill up to the bridge over the Neman, then I passed over the bridge and went uphill by the "Funicular" to Alexot. On the way back I rode my bicycle downhill across the steep road to the bridge, then crossed the bridge and the old city, and went uphill by the other "Funicular" to my rented room. I greatly enjoyed rolling down the sloping streets, at a high speed on the bicycle. There were not many cars in Kovno, so there was no danger of being hit by one.

Apropos, according to rumors, the writer Avraham Mapu wrote his famous book "Ahavath Zion" *(The Love of Zion)* sitting on the hill of Alexot.

The end of this bicycle was, as will be told later, occurred when I used it on my abortive attempt to escape from the Germans. The first German I met took it away from me and gave it to a Lithuanian boy.

Josef, Mother and Tekhiyah with grandparents during a visit in Mariampol ~1930

At the farm of Vald family, summer 1939

Standing from left:l, Mrs.Vald,Zahava Pilvinsky, Khanan Helperin

Sitting; Shoshanah Pilvinsky, Mosheh Vald, his sister

A party at the "WIZO" committee of Kibart to Mrs. Vizhanzky and Mrs. Shatenstein to their "Aliya" to Eretz-Yisrael. 1933

Sitting from left: Savta Zisle, Dobe Stern, Bartenstein, Mother (chairwoman), Shatenstein, Vizhansky, ----, ----, ----, ----, Sarah Leibovitz

On Father's Side

My father, Yehudah-Leib Rosin, was born in a small village called Sudarg (Sudargas), which was situated on the left bank of the river Neman, about 80 km west of Kovno. The small houses in the village were built of wooden beams and thatched roofs. They were located around three sides of the market square and on the fourth side there stood the Catholic church. In the 1930's some 20-30 Jewish families lived in Sudarg. It was possible to arrive in Sudarg in summer by boat and in winter by snow sled. During the rainy season or in spring when the snows melted and the ice in the river started to move, it was almost impossible to get there.

Family Tree of Dov Berchik Rosin – Father's Side
(Compiled by Joel Alpert)

```
1  Dov ROSIN
   +  Elka UNKNOWN
   2  Izhak ROSIN (1847 Sudarg, Lithuania — 1888)
   +  Sarah Beyleh NAIVIDEL (1857 — 10 Aug 1914 Yurburg, Lithuania)
      3  Chairiva Chaya Rivka ROSIN (1880 Yurburg or, Sudarg, Lithuania )
         +  Meir ELIASHEVITZ (1870 Yurburg, Lithuania — 1941 HOLOCAUST)
            4  Shlayma ELIASHEVITZ (1903 — HOLOCAUST)
               +  Yehuda UNKNOWN
            4  Golda Leah ELIASHEVITZ (1905 — 1941 HOLOCAUST)
              +  male VERBOLOWSKI ( — poss. in HOLOCAUST)
            4  Elka ELIASHEVITZ (1917 Yurburg, Lithuania — 1941 HOLOCAUST)
               +  male LANDAU? ( — poss. in HOLOCAUST)
               5  Female LANDAU? ( — poss. in HOLOCAUST)
            4  Chaya Rochel ELIASHEVITZ (1917 — poss. in HOLOCAUST)
            4  Itzchak ELIASHEVITZ (1911 Yurburg, Lithuania —Jun 1941 HOLOCAUST)
            4  Jeine Jona ELIASHEVITZ ( — 1941 HOLOCAUST)
               +  Female UNKNOWN ( — poss. in HOLOCAUST)
               5  Unknown ELIASHEVITZ ( — poss. in HOLOCAUST)
            4  Esther ELIASHEVITZ (1915 Yurburg, Lithuania — 1941 HOLOCAUST)
               +  Fivel Sraga ESS (1912 Yurburg, Lithuania — 1941 HOLOCAUST)
      3  Leaha ROSIN (1880 Yurburg or, Sudarg, Lithuania — )
         +  Chaim MINEVICH
            4  Menashe MINEVICH ( — HOLOCAUST)
            4  Berle Dov MINEVICH ( — 12 Jul 1993 Vilna, Lithuania)
               +  Pesia Pepe MOVSON ( — 18 Dec 1995)
               5  Lila Leah MINEVICH
                  +  Alexander HABNER
                  6  Daniel HABNER
                     +  Shasha CHAVNER
               5  Fima MINEVICH
                  +  Lena UNKNOWN
                  6  Misha MINEVICH
      3  Pesha ROSIN (1880 Yurburg or, Sudarg, Lithuania — HOLOCAUST)
         +  Israel APPELBOIM ( — HOLOCAUST)
            4  Sissel Naomi APPELBOIM (1911 Yurberik, Lithuania — 1959 Israel)
               +  Henach KAPSHUD (1906 Telsit, Lithuania — 1971 Israel)
               5  Rina KAPSHUD (1939 Israel — )
                  +  Aaron WARSHAWSKI
                  6  Naomi WARSHAWSKI (1962 — )
                  6  Ronen WARSHAWSKI (1966 — )
               5  Israel KAPSHUD (1946 Israel — )
                  +  Nizza GRAUER (1951 — )
                  6  Guy KAPSHUD (1972 — )
                  6  Lior KAPSHUD (1977 — )
```

```
                    5  Ezra KAPSHUD (1934 Tel Aviv, Israel — )
                         +  Dina SHACHTEN (1936 — )
                              6  Dafna KAPSHUD (1967 Israel — )
          4  Chaike APPELBOIM ( — HOLOCAUST)
          4  Izhak APPELBOIM ( — HOLOCAUST)
    3  Ber Meyer ROSIN (1882 in Yurberik, Lithuania, or Sudarg — 1959)
          +  Fannie ORKOWSKY (1889 Odessa, Russia — 1968)
          4  Florence ROSE (1911 Duluth, MN — 1931)
          4  Milton ROSE (1913 Duluth, MN — abt 1976)
               +  Judith HARRIS
               5  Deborah ROSE
                    +  Jorge UNKNOWN (Argentina — )
                         6  Michael UNKNOWN (abt 1980 — )
                         6  Alexander UNKNOWN (1990 — )
               5  Sarah ROSE
                    +  Unknown UNKNOWN
                         6  Unknown UNKNOWN
                    +  William UNKNOWN
          4  Evelyn ROSE (1915 Duluth, MN — )
               +  Edward SCHWARTZ ( — abt 1982)
          4  Irwin Izhak ROSE (2 Sep 1916 Duluth, MN — )
               +  Dorothy LUTHER (6 Oct 1918 — )
               5  Michael ROSE (1946 — )
                    +  Sarah ROSIN
                         6  Adam ROSE (1990 — )
                         6  Daniel ROSE (1991 — )
               5  Elizabeth ROSE (4 Dec 1948 — )
                    +  Dr. Joe Dennis HULL
                         6  Alexander Ross HULL (2 Oct 1988 — )
                         6  Olivia Chelsea HULL (13 Dec 1990 — )
    3  Masha Rachel ROSIN (1888 Yurburg or, Sudarg, Lithuania — )
          +  Eliezer BASS (1896 — )
          4  Bilha BASS (1925 — )
               +  Gutman LERENTAL (1918 — )
               5  Naomi LERENTAL (1945 — )
                    +  Moshe ISRAELI
                         6  Avital ISRAELI (1974 — )
                         6  Daria ISRAELI (1976 — )
               5  Ruven LERENTAL (1949 — )
                    +  Tamar PLASHKES
                         6  Yaniv LERENTAL (1972 — )
                         6  Moran LERENTAL (1978 — )
               5  Ron Ami LERENTAL (1959 — )
                    +  Yael BRAUN
                         6  Tom LERENTAL (1990 — )
                         6  Dor LERENTAL (1993 — )
    3  Hillel Mordechai ROSIN (abt 1891 Yurburg or, Sudarg, — 1941 HOLOC.)
          +  Bella UNKNOWN
          4  Child1 ROSIN
          4  Child2 ROSIN ( — poss. in HOLOCAUST)
          4  Child3 ROSIN ( — poss. in HOLOCAUST)
          4  child4 ROSIN ( — poss. in HOLOCAUST)
          4  child5 ROSIN ( — poss. in HOLOCAUST)
          4  child6 ROSIN ( — poss. in HOLOCAUST)
    3  Shlayma ROSIN (1897 Yurburg or, Sudarg, Lithuania — )
          +  Sruel Israel Moshe BRESKY
          4  Bella BRESKY (1926 — 1939)
          4  Isa Izhak BRESKY (1928 — 18 May 1994 Gorky, Russia)
               +  Tamara UNKNOWN
               5  Segej BRESKY
                    +  Female UNKNOWN
                         6  Unknown BRESKY
               5  Vova BRESKY
                    +  Female UNKNOWN
                         6  Unknown BRESKY
               +  Tonya UNKNOWN
2  Berril Bertzik Dov ROSIN (1858 — 8 Jan 1921 Sudarg, Lithuania)
```

```
     +  Dvorah Leah UNKNOWN ( — 29 Mar 1929)
  3  Meir David ROSIN (Sudarg, Lithuania — )
        +  Naomi UNKNOWN
     4  Leah ROSIN
              +  Unknown SEYMOR
              5  Daughter1 SEYMOR
              5  Daughter2 SEYMOR
              5  Daughter3 SEYMOR
  3  Morris Moshe ROSIN (1884 Sudarg, Lithuania — 1974)
        +  Fannie LEVITAS (abt 1882 — 1951)
     4  Lincoln ROSIN (1915 New York, NY — 2004)
              +  Dorothy FEIN (1913 — 2002)
              5  Ed J. ROSIN (1953 — )
                    +  Kathleen BERG (abt 1955 — )
                    6  Claire ROSIN (1983 — )
                    6  Lillie Anne ROSIN (abt 1986 — )
                    6  Charlotte ROSIN (abt 1988 — )
                    6  Camille ROSIN (abt 1994 — )
              5  Robert H. ROSIN (1943 — )
                    +  Marion LIPPMAN (1946 — )
                    6  Jonathan B. ROSIN (1970 — )
                          +  Elise LONG (abt 1963 — )
                          7  Cameron Jordan ROSIN (1997 — )
                          7  Spencer Justin ROSIN (2000 — )
              5  Nan ROSIN (1946 — )
                    +  Mark HARRIS (1946 — )
                    6  Melissa Hope HARRIS (abt 1974 — )
                    +  Joseph GARTENBERG ( — abt 2001)
        +  Cele DENGROVE ( — 1988)
  3  Frank Mordechai ROSIN (Sudarg, Lithuania — poss. in Dallas, TX)
        +  Rose COHEN (Waco, TX — )
     4  Sylvia ROSIN (1913 El Paso, TX — Feb 1998)
              +  Marcus GENDEL
              5  Loyce GENDEL (1938 — )
                    +  Edward WEITZ
                    6  Lisa Fran WEITZ (21 Jun 1960 — )
                          +  Dan SERBAN (Rumania — )
                          7  Lauren Haley SERBAN (6 Feb 1990 — )
                    6  Lane Elliot WEITZ (5 Dec 1962 — )
                          +  Cheryl KRAMER
                          7  Michael Ross WEITZ (26 Feb 1991 — )
                          7  Samuel WEITZ (25 Mar 1996 — )
                    +  David RUBIN ( — abt Jan 1997)
  3  Mina ROSIN (Sudarg, Lithuania — 1941 Sudarg, Lithuania, HOLOCAUST)
        +  Dov HILELSON ( — bef 1935)
     4  Shlomo HILELSON ( — 1941 Sudarg, Lithuania, HOLOCAUST)
     4  Chaya Anna HILELSON
              +  Jack COHEN
              5  Ben D. COHEN
              5  Lia COHEN
                    +  male ZIMMERMAN
                    6  David ZIMMERMAN
              5  Dorothy COHEN
                    +  male GOULD
                    6  Sheryl GOULD
     4  Namiel Nachman Nate HILELSON (1902 Sudarg, Lithuania — abt 1976)
              +  Pauline UNKNOWN ( — 1992)
              5  Jennie Lee HILLSON
                    +  Unknown STEPHENSON
                    6  Cara STEPHENSON
                    6  Gregg STEPHENSON
                    +  Jim ROBINSON
                    6  Cara ROBINSON
                          +  male ARNOULD
              5  David HILLSON
                    +  Rebecca S. UNKNOWN
                    6  Nathan HILLSON
```

```
                    6  Bethany HILLSON (abt 1980 — )
                +  Eileen GREVEY
      4  Yitzhak HILELSON ( — 1995 Tel Aviv, Israel)
          +  Female UNKNOWN ( — bef 1945 Kovno Ghetto, HOLOCAUST)
          5  Son HILELSON ( — bef 1945 Kovno Ghetto, HOLOCAUST)
          +  Chaja CHAZANOWITZ ( — 1995 Tel Aviv, Israel)
          5  David HILELSON
              +  Gila UNKNOWN
                  6  Rachel HILELSON
                  6  Dor HILELSON
                  6  Yitzhak HILELSON (Jan 1997 — )
      4  Jack Yakov Albert HILELSON (16 Jan 1907 — 10 Oct 1983)
          +  Helen Esther PEARL (10 Aug 1909 — 1 Oct 2004)
          5  Nancy Ruth HILLSON (21 Feb 1937 — )
              +  Leopold Ivan ZENNER (5 Aug 1933 — )
                  6  Lori Dianne ZENNER (28 Nov 1963 — )
                      +  Bradley Steven MARCUS (1 May 1956 — )
                          7  Lindsay Jordan MARCUS (23 Dec 1993 — )
                  6  Lisa ZENNER (9 Apr 1960 — )
                      +  Steve Carl MAGER (13 Jan 1954 — )
                          7  Lauren Alison MAGER (15 Mar 1981 — )
                          7  Julianne Alyssa MAGER (11 Jun 1985 — )
                          7  Meghan Elyse MAGER (20 May 1988 — )
                  6  David Michael ZENNER (27 Dec 1969 — )
                      +  Elisa KAHN
                          7  Jacob Ryan ZENNER (2 Feb 2000 — )
                          7  Emily Aerin ZENNER (7 Jun 2002 — )
              +  Eileen GREVEY
          5  Sylvia HILLSON (16 Jan 1936 — )
              +  Jacob GILON (Israel — )
                  6  Elizabeth Susan GILON (Jun 1960 — )
      4  Henry Hillel HILELSON ( — 1991)
          +  Ruth FRIEDMAN ( — 1993)
          5  Charlotte HILLSON (abt 1943 — abt 1995)
              +  Elvin KANTER (abt 1929 — )
                  6  Deborah KANTER (abt 1962 — )
                  +  male UNKNOWN
                  6  Dana KANTER (abt 1964 — )
                  +  John T. L. GRUBESIC
                  6  Steven KANTER (abt 1968 — )
          5  Marietta Sissy HILLSON
              +  Stuart BERNTHOL
                  6  Lora BERNTHOL
                  6  Jason H. BERNTHOL
      4  Elka HILELSON ( — 1941 Sudarg, Lithuania, HOLOCAUST)
          +  Yehuda GOLDBERG ( — 1941 Sudarg, Lithuania, HOLOCAUST)
          5  Leah GOLDBERG ( — 1941 Sudarg, Lithuania, HOLOCAUST)
      4  Leib Aryeh HILELSON (bap. Sudarg, Lithuania — )
          +  Tzila MORDHOVICH (1918 Solokai, Zarasai District, Lith.)
      4  Gershon HILELSON(1913 Sudarg,Lith.—22 Oct 1996 Montreal,Canada)
          +  Tzila MORDHOVICH (1918 Solokai, Zarasai District, Lith.)
          5  Fania HILELSON (12 Mar 1947 Kovno, Lithuania — )
              +  Michael JIVOTOVSKY (26 Jan 1939 Moscow — )
                  6  Anath JIVOTOVSKY (23 Jun 1976 Tel Aviv — )
                  6  Leor JIVOTOVSKY (4 Aug 1975 Tel Aviv, Israel—)
          5  Moshe HILELSON (12 Mar 1947 Kovno, Lithuania — )
              +  Dina PODOLSKY (Moscow — )
                  6  Keren HILELSON (1983 Israel — )
                  6  Liat HILELSON (1983 Israel — )
    3  Yehuda Leib ROSIN (Sudarg, Lithuania — 7 Jul 1941 Kybartai, Lith.)
      +  Chaya LIEBOVITZ ( — 11 Sep 1941 Kybartai, Lithuania, HOLOCAUST)
      4  Josef ROSIN (24 Jan 1922 Kybartai, Lithuania — )
          +  Pnina CYPKIEVITZ (Wloclawek, Poland — )
          5  Amikam M ROSIN (11 May 1946 Beit-Zera, Israel — )
              +  Irith OHER
                  6  Sharon ROSIN (1972 Israel — )
                  6  Gil ROSIN (1975 Israel — )
```

```
5  Eliya ROSIN (24 Jul 1959 Haifa, Israel — )
      +  Amir VEG
         6  Inbar VEG (6 Feb 1988 — )
      +  Zvi TOREN
         6  Leor TOREN (19 Jun 1995 — )
4  Tchiya ROSIN (abt 1925 Kybartai, Lith. — 11 Sep 1941 Kybartai)
```

On Father's side

Bertzik and Leah Rosin
- Meir-David —— Leah Seymor —— 3 daughters
- Moshe-Moris —— Lincoln
  - Robert —— Jonathan
  - Nan —— Melissa
  - Eddie
    - Camille
    - Claire
    - Lilly
    - Charlotte
- Mordechai-Frank —— Sylvia Gendel —— Loyce-Leah Weitz
  - Lane
  - Lisa Serban
- Mina Hilelson
  - Shlomo
  - Chaya Cohen —— Ben
    - Lia Zimmerman —— David
    - Dorothy Gould —— Sheril
  - Nachman-Nate —— Jennie Lee Robinson
    - Cara Stephe
    - Gregg Steph
    - David Hilson —— Nathan / Bethany
  - Yitzchak —— David —— Rachel / Dor
  - Yakov-Jack —— Nancy Zenner —— Lori / Lisa / David
    - Sylvia Gilon —— Elizabeth
  - Hilel-Henry —— Charlotte Kanter —— Debora / Dana Grubesi / Steven
    - Marietta Bernthol —— Lora / Jason
  - Ella Goldberg —— Leah
  - Aryeh
  - Gershon —— Fania Jivotovsky —— Anath / Leor
    - Moshe Hilelson —— Keren / Liath
- Yehuda-Leib Rosin —— Joseph
  - Amikam —— Sharon / Gil
  - Eliya —— Inbar
  - Tchiya

Lior

Grandpa, Grandma and the Uncles

Over the years I learned new details about my father's family, of which I was not aware when writing my memoirs. My relative and friend Joel Alpert, an an electrical engineer at MIT Lincoln Laboratory in Lexington Massachusetts, USA, whose grandfather on his mother's side came to America from Yurburg, Lithuania, carried out extensive research on the genealogy of his family and thanks to him I acquired the following details.

My great grandmother was Elka (nee?) the wife of Dov Rosin. Before being widowed she gave birth to two sons: the first Yitskhak and the second Dov-Ber (Bertchik), my grandfather, who was born after his father died.

According to a photo taken in the cemetery in Sudarg, which I received about two years ago, the name "Dov ben Dov" is embossed on his tombstone, which means that he was named after his dead father. As is well known, East European Jews didn't name a new born child after a living relative.

Grandpa's mother Elka was still a young widow and she married again, this time a widower in Yurburg named Hillel Naividel, who had two sons and three daughters from his first wife, and then another daughter with Elka named Peshe. Hillel Naividel was Joel Alpert's great-great grandfather (Specifically, Joel's maternal grandmother's grandfather).

Yitskhak Rosin, grandpa's brother, married one of Hillel Naividel's daughters, Sarah-Beile, and moved from Sudarg to Yurburg. At the Yurburg Jewish cemetery a photo of Sarah-Beile's tombstone was taken several years ago (see photo). They had two sons, Meir and Hillel and five daughters: Khayah-Rivkah Elyashevitz, Masha-Rachel (and Eliezer) Bass, Leah (and Khayim) Minevitz, Peshe Apelbaum and Shulamith (Shleime) Bresky. All these people were cousins of my father. I met Hillel Rosin, who lived in Yurburg and owned a bakery, on one occasion when I was going with my father to Sudarg. He and his family were murdered in the Holocaust. I have no knowledge about Meir nor of the family of my great grandfather Dov. Did he have any brothers? In the last years I have been receiving inquiries through the Internet from offspring of former Lithuanian Jews, who are scattered all over the world, whose surname is Rosin, asking if I am one of their relatives.

The towns of their origin are in an area not far from Yurburg, so if it was possible to go back not more than two hundred years, we could check family relations. But to my regret there is nobody left to ask. More than one hundred people of our family were murdered in the Holocaust.

Living in Israel today are my second cousin Bilhah Bass-Lerental in Benei-Brak, granddaughter of Yitskhak and Sarah-Beile Rosin and my third cousin Fima Minevitz in Ma'aloth, great grandson of Yitskhak and Sarah-Beile Rosin. Bilhah is a sculptor and has two married sons. Fima is married and has one son. I discovered these two relatives thanks to Joel Alpert.

My Grandpa Dov (Bertchik) Rosin married Devorah-Leah (nee ?) *(See "The Family Tree" up to grandchildren of my cousins)*. They lived in Sudarg and had four sons: Meir-David, Mosheh, Yehudah-Leib, Mordechai, and one daughter, Mina. Meir-David immigrated to South Africa, married and had one daughter named Leah, who lives in Johannesburg with her family.

Mosheh and Mordechai immigrated to America. Mosheh (Morris) lived his entire life in New York and was in the clothing business. He died a few years ago at the age of about 90. He had one son Lincoln, who was born in approximatly 1914. He is a lawyer and lives with his wife in Manhattan. There are two sons and one daughter. Peninah and I, together with our son Ami and his family, visited Lincoln in the 1980's during one of our visits to America. (He has since passed away).

Aunt Mina Rosin-Hilelson with a part of her family
Standing from left: Yehudah Goldberg, Leah'le, Gershon, Yits'hak
Sitting: Elka Hilelson-Goldberg, Mina, Leah-Yits'hak's wife

Uncle Mordehai (Frank) Rosin with his wife and granddaughter Loyce Gendel

Uncle Moshe (Moris) Rosin, his wife and his son's Lincoln's daughter

Uncle Meir-David Rosin with his wife Naomi

Mordechai lived in New Mexico and had one daughter named Sylvia, who lives in Dallas, Texas. She was married to Mr. Gendel and has one daughter Lois *(Leah),* who is married to Mr. Weitz. They have one married son and one married daughter. They are the owners of the well-known antiques store "Mannheim" in Dallas. Penina and I visited them in the summer of 1989. Sylvia has since passed away, Loyce divorced her husband and the antiques shop no longer belongs to the family.

I briefly met only one of my uncles. With the help of friends in South Africa I found my Uncle Meir David. I have a few letters, which he and his wife Naomi wrote to me in the early1950's.

Aunt Mina married Dov Hilelson. They had seven sons and two daughters. The sons' names were: Shelomoh, Nachman *(Namiel or Nate),* Hillel *(Henry),* Yakov *(Jack),* Leib *(Arye),* Yitskhak and Gershon. The daughters were Khayah and Elka. Grandpa Bertchik had a grocery store which he left to his son- in- law Dov Hilelson. Grandpa participated in the wedding of my parents and his photo appears in the picture of this wedding. I neither knew him or Grandma. He died in 1921 and Grandma in 1929 *(see photos of their tombstones).*

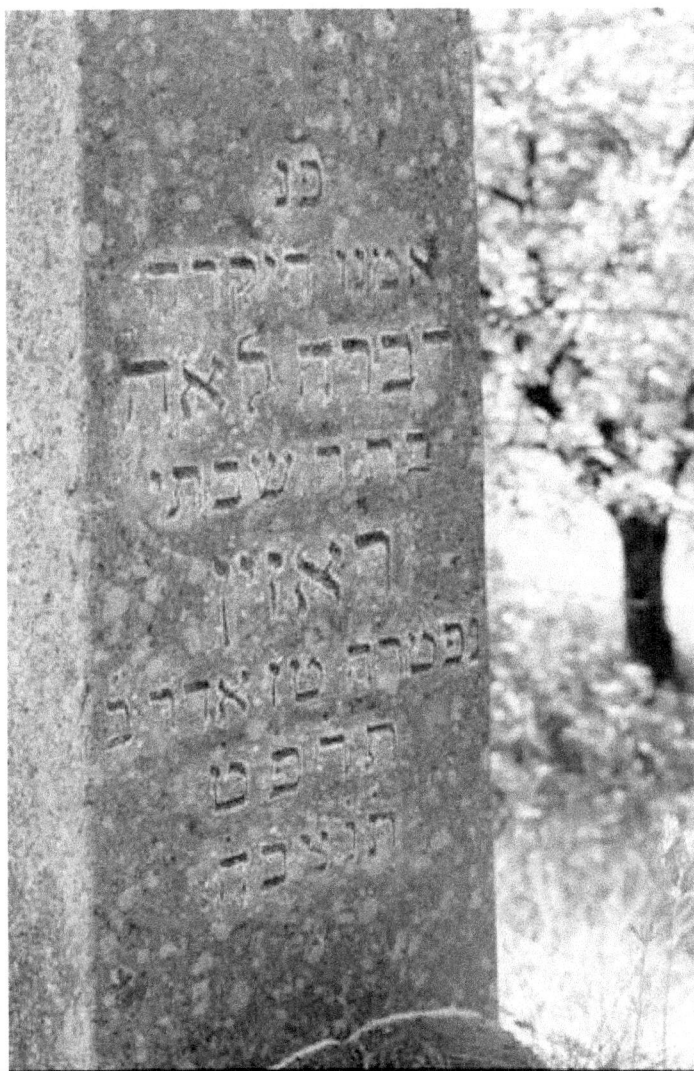

Devorah-Leah bath Shabtai Rosin (1929)

Headstone for Dov ben Dov Rosin (1921)

"In this place on the 11th of July 1941
the Hitler occupants murdered 56 of
Sudarg residents   (Jewish)
40 women and 16 children"

This inscription is written in Lithuanian during the Soviet Rule not marking
that the victims were Jews.

(Peshe Naividel-Zapolsky)

(Stepsister of Josef's Grandfather Dov Rosin)

Sarah-Beile Rosin

(Yits'hak Rosin's wife)

My Uncle Dov and my Aunt Mina I knew well, also my cousins Shelomoh, Aryeh, Yitskhak, Gershon and Elka. My uncle died when I was a little boy.

Aunt Mina, Shelomoh, Elka, her husband Yehudah Goldberg and their little girl Leah were murdered, together with all the Jews from Sudarg, in the summer of 1941. The brothers Aryeh and Gershon worked in Kovno before the war. When the invasion of the German Army into Lithuania began, they managed to escape to Russia. There they were drafted into the Lithuanian Division of the Red Army. Aryeh was killed in battle and Gershon was wounded and remained disabled. Now he lives with his wife, Arye's widow, their married twins Fania and Mosheh in Montreal, Canada. Gershon and Tsilah are not with us anymore.

Yitskhak married shortly before the war. After the German occupation of Lithuania in June 1941 he, his wife and their baby son were imprisoned in the Kovno Ghetto. His wife and his little son perished there. When the last Jews of the Kovno Ghetto were transported to the concentration camps in Germany in July 1944, Yitskhak jumped from the train and hid in the woods, not far from Sudarg, where a Lithuanian friend provided him with food. After the war he married again and now lives in Tel Aviv with his wife. They have one married son David, who lives in Ramath-Gan.

Yitskhak and his wife Khayah nee Khazanovitz passed away a few years ago. The first time I met Hillel (Henry) was when he visited Israel. Peninah and I visited him in his house in Albuquerque, in 1981. There I also met my cousin Khayah Hilelson-Cohen, who appears in the wedding picture of my parents. She told me that before she immigrated to America she hugged me, then a baby, in her arms. She has one son and two married daughters. In Albuquerque, the family of the late Nachman, his non-Jewish wife and their son and daughter live. Yakov (Jack) lived in Las Vegas (New Mexico), and I never met him. He has since passed away, after visiting Israel with his wife Helen in the summer of 1983. All the American cousins changed the family name Hilelson to Hillson.

Aunt Mina Rosin-Hilelson

Nakhman (Namiel) Hilelson
with his wife

Tsila and Gershon Hilelson

Fania Hilelson-Jivotovsky,
husband Michael, daughter Anath
and son Lior

Standing from left: Uncle Mosheh (Morris) Rosin, his second wife Tsela, Robert-Lincoln's son, Dorothy-Lincoln's wife, Lincoln-Moris's son.

From left: Eduard Weitz, Loyce (Leah) Gendel, Sylvia Rosin-Gendel, Lane Weitz, Lisa Weitz-Serban, Dan Serban.

In our family album there were pictures of all the sons and daughters of the Hilelson family, also of Uncle Mosheh with his wife. I can see these pictures clearly in my mind's eyes, but as happened to all our property, this album also got lost in the Holocaust. All the pictures from Father's side in this book I received from my cousin Sylvia Rosin-Gendel in Dallas.

We were very close with Aunt Mina and her sons. They were nice people and I liked them very much. Several times in the summer, Father and I went to Sudarg for vacation. The village was situated on a high hill surrounded by groves and at the foot of it flowed the river Neman. We liked to sit in a grove on the hill overlooking the river, where it was tranquil and the air was clear. I read Yiddish books aloud for Father, since his eyesight was bad.

The trip to Sudarg was a complicated endeavor. First, we went by train to Kovno. There we stayed overnight at Father's good friends, the Khaimovitz family. Next morning we sailed to Sudarg by boat, on the river Neman. The trip lasted for six to eight hours. As a young boy this was an exciting experience for me.

Father was a modest man, not a speechmaker and did not like to be involved too much in communal business. He was a learned man, who acquired his knowledge it seems to me, by himself. He knew Yiddish, Hebrew, Russian, a little German and a little Lithuanian. He was familiar with Russian literature and liked to cite Gogol and Goncharov. The letters he sent to Uncle Barukh in Tel Aviv were written in Yiddish, but I have a few letters he wrote in excellent Hebrew. *Table 8* shows a moving letter written by him in Hebrew in which he tells Barukh about the death of his father. The other Yiddish letters are discussing on his decision to immigrate to Eretz-Yisrael despite the difficulties and the measures he needed take to reach his objective.

Once, when I was a little boy, I quizzed Father, using a Hebrew dictionary and was impressed with his knowledge. In the year 1922, a chapter of the "Tarbuth" *(Culture)* organization was founded in Kibart, in which Father was one of the six members of its board. The slogan of this organization was: "The People of Yisrael, the Land of Yisrael and the Language of Yisrael." The Kibart chapter appealed to the "Vaad Hakehilah" *(Community Committee)* to allocate it a monthly sum as to support its budget. My father was one of the men who signed this letter which was written in Hebrew.

Father had a fine sense of humor, and some of the jokes and wise sayings I heard from him I still repeat now. He was a good man and, according to Mother, if he had been a woman, he would have had a house full of bastards, because he could not say "no." I remember several times, that he signed for friends as a guarantor on promissory notes and later on paid their debts.

The only public job Father agreed to accept was to represent the "Keren Hayesod" *(Jewish Foundation Fund)* in Kibart. Once a year its agent came from the Central Office of the Fund in Kovno (Eliezer Rozentsvaig), made a speech and raised money for the Fund with the aid of my Father.

In our store we sold various kinds of paper, cardboard, assorted pencils and pens, ink, Indian ink, rope. The good pencils, the fountain pens (Pelican, Hardtmuth exist even now) and rope we imported from Germany. The rope factory's agent was a German from Eydtkuhnen, who was a bachelor and had a sweetheart in Kibart. He came to our store very often and was a friend of our family. Once, when Father and Mother went to Kovno for the day, he came to our store and helped me wait on the customers. For my "Bar Mitzvah" he bought me a pocketknife. I assume that this friendship lasted at least until 1936, by which time the Nazi regime reigned firmly in Germany.

From time to time, Father would travel to the small towns in the vicinity, in order to collect orders from merchants for the goods we sold. After returning home, he would make up the goods into parcels and send them to customers. Whenever possible I helped Father in this job. Mother also helped a lot in the store. There were times when we employed outside help in the store. When I was very young this help was my cousin Aryeh Hilelson, later it was Yosef Bartenstein, until his immigration to Eretz-Yisrael. Opposite our store, across the street, there was the Government Elementary School. At the beginning of the school year my help in the store was important, because of the many children and their parents who came to buy copybooks, pencils etc.

Once, at the age of 12 or 13, I found a box with small harmonicas, each with eight tones, in the store. I had a good ear for music, and so I tried to play simple melodies. I found two Jewish boys in town, who knew how to play harmonicas and they taught me its technique. I only bought a real harmonica after earning my first money from lessons in mathematics I gave to a girl from a high school. It was then that I started to practice playing and I advanced well, as will be told later.

In the summer of 1940, when Lithuania became a Soviet Republic, most of the stores and factories in Kibart were nationalized. In each of them a manager was appointed, either someone who had been an illegal communist before, or somebody now freed from jail, having been imprisoned for being a communist. Among them there were many Jews. Our store was too small and therefore not nationalized, so Father continued to run it. The Soviet soldiers, who were staying in Kibart, bought almost everything we had in the store, even some merchandise from the stockroom, where it had been stored without use for years.

My sister Tekhiyah was three years younger than me. She studied in the Hebrew Elementary School (six grades) in Kibart and graduated in 1938. After that she studied in the Hebrew Progymnasium in Virbalis for three years and, when this school was closed by the Soviets in 1940, she began to study in the Government High School in Kibart. She was a lovely girl and a good student. In Table 7 there is a short letter Tekhiyah wrote to Avraham at the age of 10 in Hebrew describing her feelings when I fell ill.

I do not remember much about her, maybe because in all the years when she changed from a little girl into a young and lovely woman, I was mostly not at home and busy with my own concerns. From 1936 until 1939 I studied in the Hebrew High School in Mariampol and during the years 1940-41 at the University in Kovno. Tekhiyah had her own friends and I regarded her as a little girl. The difference of three years between us was very significant during this stage of our lives. Tekhiyah and Mother were murdered in July 1941 when she was 16 years old.

Tekhiyah with our cousins Yitskhak, Aryeh and Gershon, 1940

We kept a traditional Jewish home. There were different sets of dishes for milk and meat products and parallel sets for "Pesakh." Before "Pesakh" the glass dishes were immersed in a tub of water to make them "Kosher" for "Pesakh." All holidays were celebrated according to tradition and with specialty dishes prepared by Mother for each Holiday. Mother used to bake the Shabath "Khallah" herself and prepare "gefillte" fish. She lit candles on Friday night. We ate these delicious dishes with great pleasure, but in the years I remember we didn't get soup or meat, as was common in years before. On Shabath and holidays, Father went to the synagogue, where he had a permanent place which was rented a year ahead. On Yom Kippur we fasted. The "Seder" was held according to all the rules. I went to the synagogue every time Father did. Only when I was 14 years old did I stop and my parents did not force me to continue.

My parents bought the "Shekel," recognized as a membership card of the Zionist Organization. It entitled them to vote in the elections, which also took

place in Lithuania, at Zionist Congresses.

We used to receive periodicals from Eretz-Yisrael, such as "HaPoel HaTsair" etc. For me, my parents subscribed to the youth journal "Itoneinu" *(Our Newspaper)*. A few times I solved some of the puzzles in that journal with Mother's help, and as a reward I got several books sent to me from Eretz- Yisrael. It was a great experience for me.

For some reason, maybe due to income tax problems, we did not have a telephone, either in our apartment or in our store. We bought a radio made by "Siera" of Holland in 1938. Mother's cousin, Esther Telshitz-Gidansky, who, after escaping in 1939 from Nazi occupied Memel, lived with us for some time, introduced me to classical music, which was broadcast on the radio. Before that I knew very little about this subject.

1938 Graduation class of the Hebrew Elementary School,
Above: Headmaster A.Varshavsky, representative of the parents
committee Meir Leibovitz
At the right side: Tekhiyah and Elyakim

Chapter 3: The Years of Childhood and Education in Elementary and High School   (1928-1939)

From my childhood I remember a few events that happened when I was six or eight years old. One summer day, my friend David Shadkhanovitz and I came running into the backyard of our house. We saw a cat and threw stones at it, but David's stone, instead of hitting the cat, hit my head. We tried to stop the bleeding of the wound on my head but did not succeed. We were scared, and so we went to my Mother, telling her that a cat had dislodged a stone from the roof, which then had hit my head. When mother started to attend to my wound, David fainted, and the truth was revealed.

Near our backyard, a pile of sand had been dumped for some purpose. Usually children of the neighborhood came to play on it. Once I pushed a child, he fell on to the sand and bit his tongue so badly, that it was necessary to have it stitched. The child's parents were poor, so my parents paid for all his medical treatment, as medical insurance did not exist at that time.

During these years, motor cars fanned our imagination. Only a few could be seen in Kibart. In the store, in our backyard, there were wooden boxes of different sizes. My friend David and I, sometimes with the help of other children, built "Busses" with those boxes. It was an exciting game, into which we invested much energy and time. The roof of the "Bus" was built with the big heavy signs of liquidated stores, which were made of metal sheets with wooden frames. It was a great pleasure to sit in the "Bus," especially when it was raining outside. Once David climbed onto the roof of the "Bus" to locate the cracks through which water seeped into the "Bus." The roof collapsed, the heavy signs pressed onto his belly and he could not get out. His mother, who was standing on the balcony of their kitchen, heard his shouts for help and alarmed the housekeeper, who came running and freed him from the oppressive weight. As a result, we were not allowed to get anymore boxes to play with. I would like to point out that we never played with Lithuanian children. We were a little afraid of the "Shkotzim," who always oppressed us.

The Elementary School

In the Elementary School, there were two preparatory classes and four regular classes. After completing that school, it was possible to enter the third class of the high school and to study for six more years. It necessitated twelve years of learning to get the matriculation certificate. One entered the Elementary School at the age of seven.

At the age of seven or eight, I joined the "HaShomer HaTsair" youth organization. The "Maon" *(Den, dwelling)* of the organization was near our house, so with my parents' permission, I became a "Khabir," as the youngsters were called.

The "HaShomer HaTsair" organization in Lithuania was called "The Hebrew Scout Organization HaShomer HaTsair," because the semi Fascist regime in Lithuania would not permit the activity of a socialist movement in its state. We wore the scout uniform with all scouting emblems and our activity centered on scouting and Zionism. My cousin Avraham Ben Yehuda (Leibovitz), who was very active in the Kibart branch of the organization before his "Aliyah" to Eretz-Yisrael, established strong ties with the Lithuanian scouts in Kibart. I remember the visit of a delegate of the movement from Eretz-Yisrael, Aviva Tager from Kibbutz Ma'abaroth. She was the first Jew I met who did not speak Yiddish. She was born in Bulgaria, where Jews were of Sefardi origin and did not know Yiddish. Until then I thought that every Jew spoke Yiddish.

Kibart branch of "HaShomer-HaTsair"~ 1933

First line from left:------,Imanuel Volchansky, the Flag, Mosheh Khlamnovitz, ----Sarah Yofe
Second line: Max Vizhansky, David Levin, Hayim Borohovitz, Yehiel Feferman, Dov Shtern, Esther Ozerov, Yosef Bartenshtein, Avraham Leibovitz, Yafah Froman,-----, Nehamah Levin
Third line:Tehiyah Rosin, Sarah Mandelblat, Doba-----, Yerakhmiel Yofe, Fruma Saharovitz, Shalom Vidomliansky, Boba Borovik, -----
Fourth line from left: Zalman Epshtein. From right: Miriam Landau, Yenta Levin
Fifth line: Mihael Davidson, the fifth: Yitshak Zaharik

A group of Kibart youth 1940
Standing from left: Sarah-Bluma Zilbersky, "Khaluts" refugee from Poland
Second line: Aryeh Leibovitz, Miriam "Khalutsa" from Poland, Josef Rosin
Third line: ____, Mosheh Khlamnovitz, Rachel Vilensky

I remember what happened in the Elementary School, as regards my talents as an actor. When I was in the first or second grade, a musical was prepared for the Hanukah party. I got the role of a teacher and had to act and sing. In the middle of rehearsals the director dismissed me from the show because of lack of talent. I was, of course, very offended, even the intervention of my mother did not help, and I was out of the musical. Ever since that time I have never acted in any play. My lack of acting talent can be evaluated in different ways, depending on one's point of view. I always say what I think, without acting.

In the Elementary School I studied for only two years and a few months, in the second preparatory class for a few months and in the first and second regular classes for two full years. In third grade I did not go to school, but instead received lessons from private teachers, with the purpose of skipping a grade to enter fourth class in the Hebrew High School in Virbalis. My teacher on all subjects was Arye Varshavsky (now Bar-Shavit), who was the principal of the Hebrew Elementary School. During World War II he was in Russia and served as a soldier in the Lithuanian Division of the Red Army. He was injured in battle and is handicapped on one hand. After the war he came to Israel and, with the help of my Uncle Barukh, got a job, first as a teacher and later as the principal of a school in Ramat Hasharon. He had no certificates, due to all the troubles he went through during the war, with which to prove his position as the principal of the school in Kibart. My Uncle had a photo of the graduation class in 1938 in which my sister Tekhiyah and her cousin Elyakim Leibovitz appear, as well as A. Varshavsky as the principal of the school. So this photograph proved Mr. Varshavsky's story about himself.

The High School

At the beginning of the school year, 1933-34, I was accepted into the fourth class of the Hebrew High School in Virbalis. My friend David, who is four months older than me, was in the same class. The distance between our house and the school was 4.5 km. Usually we went there either by bus or by coach, a few of which were available in Kibart, but sometimes we went by foot. As mentioned before, our house was situated on the main street, so David and I waited for the bus at our house. One morning I got on to the bus and sat by a window. At this moment our maid came running from the house and brought me a cup of milk I had forgotten to drink, probably because of my excitement of the first days in High School. The bus started to move and the maid ran after it to get the empty cup back. The bus was full of pupils and also the principal of the school, who lived in Kibart. They all saw this event and many years later they reminded me of it. My friend Dov Stern, who was on this bus at the time, he now lives in Rishon Lezion, reminded me of this story a short while ago. I had already forgotten it.

Our maid, Jennie, was a German from a nearby village. She worked in our apartment for many years, until she married. She learned to speak Yiddish like one of us.

In the Virbalis High School I studied only for one year. After graduating from the 4th class in the summer of 1934, the High School was closed and turned into a Progymnasium of four classes. The reason for its closing was financial. There were not enough pupils to maintain a private High School.

Now the question arose what to do next? In the town of Vilkovishk, which was 20 km away from Kibart, there was a Hebrew High School. In Mariampol, 40 km from Kibart, there too was a Hebrew High School. My friend David went to study in the 5th grade in Mariampol. For me the problem was solved by other means, as will be related later on.

From right: Josef Rosin, Avraham Dembner and David Shadkhanovitz,
Graduates of the Mariampol Hebrew High School, at the party of its 70 year
jubilee. Tel-Aviv 1989

Uncle Barukh's Visit in Kibart

In that summer of 1934, my Uncle Barukh came from Tel Aviv to visit us. I was then 12 years old and it was my first meeting with him. Until that point I heard a lot about him from Mother and Grandmother and also read the letters he wrote many years before, when he was a pupil at the "Herzeliyah" High School. In those letters he described in detail the excursions the school made all over the country. Mother kept all those letters, beginning in 1911, the year of his "Aliyah"' and there after, in a round plywood box meant for women's hats. Most of the letters were sent by the Austrian postal service with their stamps. I read them like the adventure stories from "Mayen Read" and similar books.

Barukh had visited Lithuania previously in 1923 with his wife Yaffa and his two year old daughter Odeda. I was then one year old and on the photo I can be seen sitting on my Mother's knees. Uncle's visit in 1934 was a great event for me and for all the family. He arrived by train from Germany and we waited for him at the railway station in Kibart. The passport control was in Kovno, so he had to go there. Mother and Uncle Meir went with him to Kovno and then all came back together to Kibart. Uncle Barukh sailed from Eretz-Yisrael on the same ship as our national poet Chaim N. Bialik, who had to undergo surgery in Vienna.

During Barukh's stay with us, news arrived that Bialik had died and my Uncle eulogized him in Yiddish in the Synagogue in Kibart.

During this visit by Uncle Barukh, the plan to send my cousin Avraham to Eretz-Yisrael and also the plan for our family, including Grandma to make "Aliyah" crystallized. The plan was to get an "Aliyah Permit"' known as a "Capitalist Certificate." To get such a Certificate, it was necessary to prove to the British Mandatory Authorities that the applicant had deposited 1,000-Pound Sterling in a bank or invested this sum in some real estate. My parents remitted the above-mentioned sum to Eretz-Yisrael over a period of a few years, and with a part of it Uncle bought a parcel of land in Tel Aviv in a worker's quarter near the famous Labor Trend School, and the remainder he deposited in a bank. This money was earmarked to build a two story house on this plot, in accordance with the laws of the Tel Aviv Municipality for this quarter.

According to Lithuanian law one was allowed to send abroad only five Pounds per month, but the process of sending the money to Eretz-Yisrael was speeded up by the help of our German friend from Eydtkuhnen, who sent the money he received from father to Eretz-Yisrael via Germany.

Due to this plan for our "Aliyah," it was decided in the family that I take private lessons, in line with the curriculum of the "Herzeliyah" High School. Uncle Barukh sent the appropriate books and I started to learn in the autumn of 1934 according to that curriculum. I studied until the summer of 1936 with the help of several teachers. Mr. Yaffe from Virbalis taught me Hebrew, History and the Bible. Miss Sheinzon, the daughter of the "Shokhet" and cantor in Kibart, taught me English and Mr. Varshavsky, who was mentioned above, taught me the natural sciences. During those two years I read many Hebrew and Yiddish books. I was an instructor in "HaShomer-HaTsair" and also helped Father in the store.

Two days after my cousin Avraham left Kibart for his "Aliyah," I became ill with meningitis. I developed a high fever, a terrible headache and lost consciousness. My parents notified several doctors and Dr. L. Kagansky from Virbalis recommended that I be driven urgently to the Jewish Hospital in Kovno. There the illness was diagnosed and after a few weeks in the hospital, I returned home healthy and unharmed. I still remember how the doctors removed some liquid from my spine with a long needle which was introduced between the vertebrae and how it hurt. Sometimes they inserted the needle several times, because they did not find the right place and this was very unpleasant. But all's well that ends well.

For my "Bar Mitzvah" Uncle Barukh sent me a "Drashah" *(Bar Mitzvah Sermon)* which was based on the "Torah." Saturday before my birthday, 24 of Teveth *(according to the Jewish Calendar)*, I was called up to the reading of the law in the great Synagogue and read it in the Sephardi pronunciation for the first time in Kibart. *(The Ashkenazi pronunciation was the common one)*. After the prayer the guests came to our apartment. There they drank "Lekhayim" and were served refreshments which included, among other things, chopped herring and pickled roasted geese. I recited my "Sermon" to our guests and got many presents, mostly books. Checks were not a customary present in those times. After that Uncle Meir sang the then popular song in Yiddish "Do you know the land" where, among other verses, one sang "where the goats eat carobs like bread."

In the spring of 1936 we received the "Aliyah Permit," which included Grandma. Now we had to get the Visas from the British Consulate in Kovno. In a letter sent to Barukh in May 1936, Father complained that the British Consul was making it difficult to obtain the Visas. The Consul demands verifications that the money (the 1,000 Pounds) had actually been transferred to Eretz-Yisrael by Father, as it had not been deposited by Barukh in Father's name.

The "Aliyah Permit" was valid until September 1, 1936. By this date we had to be in Eretz-Yisrael. In the spring of 1936, the so called "Arab Uprising" and terror started, raging through the country resulting in many victims. From the letter my parents wrote to Barukh in May 1936 it becomes clear that, in spite of the store being almost liquidated and everything else ready for "Aliyah," they hesitated because of the terror in the country, and so our "Aliyah" was postponed.

I received the letters Father and Mother wrote to Barukh during these years, which he had saved, only after he passed away. According to these letters it seems, that he had been too slow dealing with our issues and possibly as a result of this our "Aliyah" was postponed, thus causing the tragic consequences.

Since we did not leave Lithuania by September 1st, my parents became worried about my education.

In Mariampol (September 1936-June 1939)

There were two alternatives, as mentioned before, the Hebrew High Schools in Vilkovishk or in Mariampol. Finally my parents decided to send me to Mariampol, because we knew the principal of the school there, who previously was a teacher at the High School in Virbalis, and my friend David Shadkhanovitz, who had studied there a year before, promised to help me integrate into the new circle of friends.

During the two previous years, when I was taught by private teachers according to the curriculum of the "Herzeliyah" school, I did not learn the obligatory subjects which were taught in the High Schools in Lithuania, such as Lithuanian, German, Latin and Lithuanian History. Mother went to Mariampol for a talk with the principal of the school, and it was decided that I be accepted into the 6th grade, and that during my studies there I would have to complement the missing parts of the above-mentioned subjects. I did so with the help of private teachers. The Lithuanian language was taught to me by a pupil of a high class in one of the Lithuanian schools, who was recommended by our Lithuanian teacher. The teachers of our school taught me the other subjects in the evenings. After a few hard months I integrated well into my class and reached the standard level in all subjects. In the 7th and 8th grades I was already a good pupil and received my Graduation Certificate in the summer of 1939.

In the 4th grade of High School there were examinations on Nature and Geography and the marks one got were recorded in the Graduation Certificate. I did not participate in these examinations, because I intended to go to Eretz-Yisrael. For this reason I did not get the Certificate relating to the four classes of the High School in Virbalis and I had to go through those examinations in the 8th grade in Mariampol. I did not have a Graduation Certificate from the Elementary School in Kibart either, having left that school after the 3rd grade. And so it happened that the first official certificate on my studies was the Graduation Certificate of the High School.

The transition from learning for two years with private teachers to studying in the High School in a relatively big city was an exciting experience for me. In the 6th grade there were then about 20 boys and girls from Mariampol and surroundings. On "Hanukah" a dance party with refreshments was arranged in school, and the music teacher organized a small band for it. I played the violin and there were also two mandolins and a drum.

During this first year in Mariampol I lived in a room I had rented in Mrs. Popel's apartment. She was the widow of Rabbi Popel, who, until his death, was the Rabbi of Mariampol. He was well known publicly and a deputy in the Lithuanian Seim *(Parliament)*. I got lunch, with payment of course, at the house of the "Shokhet" and Cantor Lansky. There was a son, who studied in the famous "Yeshiva" in Slabodka, a suburb of Kovno; a daughter, who learned in the Hebrew High School and a baby. (*There were rumors, that when the Nazis entered Mariampol and abuses against the Jews began, the Lansky family committed suicide*). I was not satisfied with the cleanliness in their house, and so, for the next year, lunched at the restaurant of Mrs. Daniel, whose son happened to be the gym teacher in our school. I still remember the big pieces of filleted fish and the spices with garlic "Pecha" (jellied feet) I ate there.

In the 7th grade there were already fewer pupils and in the 8th grade only nine pupils were left, eight boys and one girl (Pesia Levin), who was my girlfriend. During lessons we sat together, holding hands under the bench. She was a distinguished pupil, and we did our homework together. After graduation she was accepted into the Medical Faculty of Kovno University, probably due her excellent marks in her Graduation Certificate and her success in the entrance examinations to the University. Very few Jewish pupils were accepted into this faculty. When the war began, she returned home to Mariampol and was murdered together with all the Jews of this city.

In the second year in Mariampol I lived with an old couple, Yisrael Moshe Vittenberg and his wife. He was a wise man and I liked to chat with him. Most of his time he read Yiddish journals which someone sent him from America.

In the third and last year in that city I lived with a young couple, who had married recently. He was a salesman in the big cloth store of Kushner. The apartment was on the third floor and my room in it was small, with a sloping ceiling.

All the rooms I lived in during the three years in Mariampol were situated on the main street, called Warsaw St., in Lithuanian it was called Vytauto, after their Great Prince.

The years in the High School were good and interesting. I came back to regular learning and to an active social life. Mariampol, relatively to Kibart, was a big city with many Jewish youth. Not all of them learned in the Hebrew High School, because it was a private institute and tuition fees were high. In government schools tuition fees were only symbolic, so many Jewish boys and girls learned there.

On Saturdays I was usually at home. Only when there was much homework, did I stay in Mariampol. I believe that my studying in Mariampol cost my parents a great deal of money. Actually, I had little idea if the cost was a lot or a little. I grew up protected as if living in a glasshouse. I did not worry about what I did not have, and had no idea about poverty. During the years in Mariampol, at the age of 14 to 17, I did not feel a lack of money, but in accordance with my parents' request, I was not a spendthrift.

The Hebrew High School in Mariampol was considered to be the first in Lithuania and the second in the world, after the "Herzeliyah" school in Tel Aviv. The establishment of Hebrew High Schools in independent Lithuania was largely due to the German Jews, who were the first teachers and principals of these schools. They had extensive knowledge and left a great impact on the Hebrew educational network in Lithuania. The first principal of the High School in Mariampol was Dr. Loewenherz, a German Jew, who later immigrated to Eretz-Yisrael and became the principal of the High School in Kiryath Motzkin.

Some of the older teachers in the school I attended had received their training in Russia, whereas the younger ones had studied in Lithuania. Among the senior teachers were Levin, Ayerov and Rosenbaum, and among the junior teachers I remember particularly the Math teacher Taibele Kagan, who was a lovely woman, as well as the Latin teacher, Miss Smilg. The boys in the 8th grade were 17 to 18 years old and sometimes embarrassed the young teachers and made them blush.

The teacher of the Lithuanian language was a Lithuanian named Yeshmanta, who had been teaching for many years. German was taught beginning in the 3rd grade until graduation. The teacher was Mr. Levin and Miss Vitenshtein taught in the higher classes. She was a young woman, born in Mariampol, who demanded too much from her pupils. For example, we were studying Shiller's play "The Virgin from Orleans." For homework Miss Vitenshtein gave us the assignment of recounting a few pages from this play, but in fact we had to learn them by heart. This took up much time, since there were also other subjects we had to study at the same time. One day, this happened in the 7th grade, we decided to organize a protest strike, and so on one Sunday we simply did not go to school. The first lesson on this day was with Mr. Ayerov, whom we respected very much. The second lesson was German, but when Mr. Ayerov entered an empty classroom he was very insulted, because he thought that the strike was directed against him. Only after we apologized was he satisfied that this was not so. The strike caused a big uproar in the school, but I do not remember if somebody was punished, and whether the strike made any difference as regards the German lessons.

After the final examinations were over, we organized a graduation party in the apartment of our classmate Shemuel Rosin, who was the son of the principal of the Hebrew Elementary School in Mariampol. Due to the fact that there was only one girl in our class, we invited six or seven additional Jewish girls, who studied in the Government High School in the city. It was a nice party which lasted almost until dawn, and on this occasion I said good-bye to my friends and to the school.

By the way, because of our common surname "Rosin" and the fact that we both lived in the same street, Shemuel Rosin received several love letters from a young Jewish girl, who studied in the Government High School. He was ill at the time, and did not understand what was going on. Only after he recovered did it occur to him that these letters were meant for me!!

On summing up the studies in High School, it can be said that I knew, apart from other subjects, more or less five languages: Yiddish, the vernacular of most Jews; Hebrew, which I learned for many years; German, which I heard often from my Mother, who spoke with the many Germans who lived in Kibart and in Eydtkuhnen and also from the six years I studied this language in High School. I read German freely and also speak it well enough; Lithuanian, which we studied from the second preparatory class in the Elementary School. In the upper grades in High School we studied in the Lithuanian language also Lithuanian History and Literature, as well as Latin. We were tested on these subjects for the Graduation Certificate. I can say that I knew Lithuanian well and I passed the examination with good marks, but my accent was not authentic; Latin, which we studied for four years and also take examinations for graduation. We learned the poems of Ovidius and Virgilius and the Odes of Horacius in Latin, but most of the time we studied Caesar's books "The Gaelic Wars." For the graduation examinations we had to translate one chapter of these books into Lithuanian. I started to study English during my preparations for "Aliyah," but whatever knowledge I have of this language I received during my studies at the "Technion" and during the years I worked with the "Tahal" Company. In addition my recent work in translating my Memoirs and those of Peninah's into English as well as writing articles on the Jewish communities of Lithuania in English also helped to improve my English fluency. I heard Russian at home when my parents talked to each other in this language in order that I should not understand what they were saying. I learned to read the Kirylic letters as a young boy at home. I am not saying that I know Russian well, but I am familiar with this language as a result of living under Soviet rule in Lithuania for two years and for another few months with the Soviet Partisans.

This was the destiny of many Jewish children in the Diaspora, especially in Eastern Europe, who, at the age of seven-eight years, had to know at least three languages.

Chapter 4: The University

(October 1939 - June 1941)

After finishing High School the question was what next? Our "Aliyah" had been postponed for an indefinite period therefore it became clear that I had to acquire an academic profession in Lithuania. I knew that I wanted to become an engineer, in spite of the fact that I did not know exactly what this meant. As a youngster I showed interest in various instruments so I thought I would study Mechanical Engineering. But my friend Yitskhak Rabinovitz, who started to study Civil Engineering a year before, influenced me to do the same. In the summer of 1939 I registered with the Civil Engineering Faculty of the University of Kovno, which was named after the Lithuanian Great Prince Vytautas (1350-1430). This University was the only one in Lithuania and in addition to Engineering, also had departments in the Humanities, Law and Medicine. It was obligatory for each applicant who graduated from a private High School to pass an entrance examination in Lithuanian, despite the fact that two months earlier we had passed the Government Examination in this language and its literature for the purpose of receiving the Graduation Certificate. This was one of the measures designed to make acceptance to the University more difficult for Jewish students. I took the examination, which included the writing of an essay on one of three themes, and I passed it. Tuition fees in the University were very low, 200 Lit per year, $65 according to the rate of exchange then, but the main expenses were related to living expenses including boarding and food. I rented a room together with Yitskhak Rabinovitz, with a Jewish family in the old city of Kovno, not far from the Municipality.

The many University buildings were spread all over the city. The Engineering Faculty was situated in a nice, relatively new building in a suburb of Kovno, Alexot. To get there I had to cross the bridge over the river Neman and, as mentioned before, go uphill by funicular, a cable car which ran on rails. Most of the classes took place in this building, but for some subjects we had to go to other buildings in the city.

Attending the University and life in the big city was quite a shock to me. Kovno had a population of 160,000 inhabitants, and compared to Kibart or Mariampol this was a different world. The big distances between one place and another, public transport, the opera, the ballet, the theater etc, all this changed my life entirely.

Also the method of learning in the University was very different from the one I was used to in High School. Until I got used to all the new arrangements, much time was wasted and so the first year at University was not very productive. In addition, a chauvinistic and anti-Semitic group among the Lithuanian students started to plot against the Jewish students. They circulated proclamations in the University, demanding that Jewish students should sit on the left side of the auditorium and that they should not speak Yiddish to one another and made other discriminating demands. Actually they followed the example of Polish Universities, where there were similar occurrences at this time. The Jewish students, of course, did not accept these demands and as a result clashes took place between the two groups. These incidents negatively impacted the atmosphere and disturbed my studies.

Certain general subjects, such as Physics and Chemistry, were taught to students from several faculties, in the large auditorium in Alexot. During one of the first lectures on Chemistry the above mentioned proclamations were distributed and a clash began. The professor, Joudakis was his name, a respected man from the old Russian intelligentsia, demanded to stop the clash, but nobody listened to him. He became so angry that he suffered a stroke and we did not see him again. Another event I remember happened in the big auditorium of the Faculty of Medicine, where a lecture on the obligatory subject of Military Preparation was held for students of almost all departments. During the lecture a secret message was circulated from hand to hand: "Let's put out the lights and beat the Jews." This message also reached some Jewish students, and then it was distributed among them with the aim, that once the lights were switched off, they would be prepared to defend themselves. I stood at the upper part of the auditorium, which was shaped like an amphitheater, because there were not enough seats for all. Near me stood two big guys, and I had no idea whether they were Jewish or not. After the lecture, during which nothing bad happened, these guys said to me, after having heard me speak in Yiddish, that once the lights went out, they would have beaten me because they thought I was a "Goy." My appearance was not especially Jewish, a fact I took advantage of a few times later on, as will be told later. In addition to the incidents with the Lithuanian students and the difficulties of adapting to the new circumstances, there was the problem of technical drawing. In the Mariampol High School there was no such subject, but at the University I had to create many drawings and I was not prepared for it. It took me much time to adjust to the strict requests of the teachers. So the first year at University was not very productive for me as I had much to learn and adjust to. The official student cap of the University was a white one with a green stripe around it, but most of the students wore caps of different associations or corporations. I wore a cap of dark lilac plush and on it was embroidered, with golden cord, the emblem of the "Association of Technical Students." My only contact with that association was the payment of a yearly fee. There were also several Jewish organizations with their own caps. I joined the "Association of the Zionist Socialist Students," which had its own club, where they engaged in cultural and social activities, including dance parties.

Among my friends were members of that association who survived the

Holocaust and live in Israel: Michael and Esther Glass from Kibbutz Givat-Brener, Dr. Yitskhak Kashiv, Rachel Levin and others.

During lectures I noticed that I was not able to see what was written on the blackboard well enough. I decided to visit the student's Sick Fund and before I even began to tell the doctor about my problem, he looked into my eyes and said, "trachoma." I was so shocked, that I forgot to tell him about my myopia. I informed my mother about this, she came to Kovno, and we went to the eye specialist, Dr Grinshpan, whom Mother still knew from Mariampol. He confirmed the diagnosis and examined my vision. I saw him for treatment for many months, until I recovered. Ever since that time I wore glasses because of my myopia which has not changed much over the years.

Winds of War

June 1941 was the month of the final examinations for my second year at the University. I passed all of them, except for two which were still to come. One was on Geodesy scheduled for the 21st of that month and the second was Mathematics to be held on July 5th. Meanwhile, winds of war began to blow along our borders. The British radio, the BBC, broadcast news every day about the concentration of German troops along the borders of the Soviet Union.

In the middle of June, the Soviet authorities in Lithuania began to exile people from the state to Siberia, persons who in their eyes, could not be trusted. Among them were merchants whose stores were nationalized in 1940, Zionist operatives etc. From Kibart a few families were exiled, among them the Shadkhanovitz family. My friend David Shadkhanovitz studied at that time in Vilna. He came home immediately and managed to join his mother (his father was separated) on the exile train, in spite of the fact that he himself could stay in Lithuania.

As mentioned before, our store was not nationalized, maybe because it was very small at that time or because we were not considered among the rich in Kibart, and nobody had a reason to take revenge on us. But Father was the bursar of "Keren Hayesod" in Kibart and this was a good reason for the Soviets to exile us. We were notified by a friend, who was a clerk in the Municipality in Kibart, that we were also on the list and our turn would come. Accordingly, my parents packed all the important things into suitcases and bundles. On June 15th I got a message from them to come home urgently. I packed all my things into a suitcase and came home. I left my bicycle in Kovno. The atmosphere in the town and at home was very tense. We sat and waited for our turn.

Meanwhile along came Friday the June 20th and nothing happened. In the afternoon of that day I said to my parents that it would be a pity to forego my examination on Geodesy, which had been set for Saturday morning. This was a last minute decision, as the last train for Kovno was to leave in half an hour. I took a small rucksack with the most important things and wore ankle boots with double soles. Father gave me a big sum of money, 6,000 rubles, in case we would not meet and maybe because he did not want to have big sums of money on him. Briefly and furtively I said goodbye to my parents and my sister and ran to catch the train. I would never have imagined that I would never see them again.

During this year in Kovno I lived in a room that I had rented from the Landau family, former inhabitants of Kibart. Their apartment was on the second floor of a two story house, in a quiet neighborhood on the "Green Hill." Only a few Jewish families lived in this neighborhood. There were three children in the Landau family: a girl named Miriam, my sister's age, a son David and a little girl called Malka'le. In Kibart they lived near the border and Mr. Landau dealt illegally in foreign currency and apparently made a fine living from this business. Under Soviet rule in 1940 they moved to Kovno for reasons unknown to me. After a short while, Mr. Landau was arrested and his wife was forced to let another room in their apartment. This room was occupied by a young Jewish couple, he was a refugee from Poland and she had come from Kovno. During the time Mr. Landau was in jail, his wife brought him food parcels. Near the jail she met a Lithuanian woman, who also brought parcels for her imprisoned husband, Mr. Dushauskas. In independent Lithuania he was the Chief Engineer of the Post Office. Inside the jail the two men became friends, and so did the two women outside. To this friendship we will return later on.

On Saturday, June 21st, I took the examination in Geodesy, which was considered a difficult subject, because of the strict demands of Professor General Dirmantas, who was previously the Chief of Staff of the Lithuanian Army. I passed the examination with an above average mark and I was very happy.

On this Saturday evening I met several friends, the above-mentioned Mosheh Vald, Pesia Levin and Janett Medalie, who had graduated from the Mariampol High School a year later, together with my cousin Arye Leibovitz. This was the last graduation class of the Hebrew High School in Mariampol. We spent a pleasant time together until late into the night.

Among the nine graduates of my class, these continued their studies: David Shadchanovitz, who studied Biology in Vilna University; Avraham Dembner, Ze'ev Pak, Mosheh Vald and me, who studied Civil Engineering and Pesia Levin who studied Medicine. Those who survived the war from our class were: Ze'ev Pak, David Shadchanovitz, Avraham Dembner who were in Russia during the war, and me. Pak lived in Moscow and was in charge of the Hebrew Department of the Lenin Library. He died some years ago. The others live in Israel, where they arrived after much trouble and many adventures.

Chapter 5: At War

My Attempt to Escape

On Sunday, June 22, 1941, in the early morning, the German Air Force bombed the Kovno Airport. Only much later on that morning did Stalin broadcast the official announcement, that the German Army had attacked the Soviet Union along a front of thousands of kilometers. On that Sunday we still believed that the Red Army would beat the invaders and stop them. We had been brainwashed by the propaganda about the strength of the mighty Red Army and had seen grandiose films of the parades of the Red Army in Moscow. We had no doubt of its ability to stop the invasion. Unfortunately on that same day we began to realize that something was going wrong.

At the time I was 19.5 years old and had a recruitment document. I and a few friends of mine went to the Kovno Army Headquarters in order to join up, but nobody was there. On that day I thought I would go home, but after I heard that the Germans had advanced into Lithuania, it was not possible to reach Kibart. On this day I had lunch in the same restaurant I usually ate in and did not feel any panic in the city. Only the next day, Monday, I saw that the escape from Kovno had begun. People with bundles in their hands were seen in the streets going in the direction of the railway station. After the war I realized, that on those two days, Monday and Tuesday, thousands of people, mainly Jews, managed to escape to Russia by train, via Vilna and through Latvia.

All the Soviet officials also escaped during these days from Kovno to Russia. My friend Ze'ev Pak told me when we met in Kovno after the liberation of the city in August 1944, that at the beginning of the war he joined some families of Soviet Officers who had escaped from Kovno by truck and arrived with them in Russia.

My friend Mosheh Vald and I decided, after much hesitation, to try to escape to Russia. On the morning of Tuesday or Wednesday, June 24th or 25th , we set out on our journey with one bicycle, two small rucksacks and a big sum of money. First we went to the railway station, but found that there were no more trains going anywhere. So we decided to go by foot, intermittently riding the bicycle parallel to the railway tracks heading eastwards to Vilna. We did not want to go onto the highway, because we remembered how the German planes had shot and strafed the refugees, who were escaping on the roads in Poland during the first days of the German invasion into that country. On the first day we went along the rail tracks and in the evening reached a small farm. We asked the owner's permission to sleep in the barn and paid him for the bread and milk he gave us. On the following day, early in the morning, we continued on our way and after a few hours arrived at the railway station of Koshedar (*Kaisiadorys in Lithuanian*) on the Kovno-Vilna line. A freight train with many wagons was standing there, at its head a smoking locomotive, and soldiers of the Red Army busy loading military equipment onto these trucks, which we also noticed contained artillery guns. The soldiers were working slowly without any panic and this of course raised our hopes. Meanwhile near the station carts harnessed to horses were passing, with Jewish families and their meager property, who had escaped from their burning towns. Except for my friend and myself, there were several Lithuanians in this station who also wanted to go eastwards on that train. At first, the Russian officer in charge of this train did not agree to let civilians join the train, but after much urging he gave in, and so all the civilians climbed up onto the train, including Moshe Vald, myself and my bicycle. The wagon we went up into was empty except for us and a few other civilians. At noon the train moved towards Vilna. It was a beautiful day, the sun was shining and the sky was blue, the heavy doors of the wagon were open and we sat on the floor with our feet outside. I have to confess that I was happy during these hours. This went on for some time, until the train stopped suddenly. We stood for a few hours then the train returned in the direction of Koshedar. The aim was to go from Koshedar to Yaneve *(Jonava)* and from there northwards to Shavl *(Siauliai in Lithuanian)* and Latvia. Meanwhile it was evening and with darkness we arrived in Yaneve, where we were ordered to leave the train.

This was the end of our attempt to reach Russia. As we were informed later, there were German paratroopers in the hinterland, causing much chaos. They had cut the retreat routes of the Red Army and in less than one month captured more than one million prisoners, as well as all the military equipment in the area.

Mosheh and I jumped from the train and walked far away from it. Then we lay down to sleep in a field beside some bushes. It was cold and during our troubled sleep we heard different noises on the nearby road, sounding like cars, tanks etc., but who moved on that road and in which direction, we did not know. This was the first night of many nights of nightmares, and I had no means of knowing what was still in store for me. At dawn we started on our way back to Kovno, this time too we did not use the main roads, but side roads instead. After a short while we came to a village, at the entrance of which we saw a military airfield, which had already been abandoned that day. Along the road there were small wooden houses and, if I am not mistaken, they had straw thatched roofs. We knocked on one door and asked in Lithuanian if we could get something to eat. After a short conversation with the old woman, who opened the door to us, it became clear that she spoke Yiddish and that in this village there lived many Jewish farmers. She fed us and when she heard that we were on our way to Kovno, she directed us to a two story house further along the street, which belonged to a wealthier and socially higher placed Jewish family. The members of this family put an end to our plans to continue on to Kovno, advising us not to go on to there now, because in the suburb of Slabodka the Lithuanians had carried out a terrible "Pogrom," in which about one thousand Jews were murdered in one night by the cruelest of means. They got this news from a Lithuanian neighbor, who had been sent by them to Kovno in order to ascertain what was going on there.

The Way Back

After staying several days with these kind Jewish people, during which time more refugees had arrived at this house, we decided nevertheless to continue our journey to Kovno. We walked on paths through the many woods in this area. We smelled the odor of corpses and saw footprints of shoes we had never seen before, which we presumed to be from German paratroopers. We went along a path for a few hours and then had to cross a road before continuing on the same path on the other side of the road. When we came to the road, a German officer appeared before us, surrounded by several Lithuanian youngsters who had white stripes on their arms. When they saw us they said something to the German and he immediately called us. We approached him and he said, "We need this bicycle." Of course, we did not argue with him. We took off our rucksacks from the bicycle and gave it to the Lithuanian man, who had wanted it for himself. This was my first meeting with a German serviceman, which this time had ended only with the robbery of my bicycle. We loaded the rucksacks on our backs and continued on our way. Later we met a group of five to six Jewish youngsters and among them two girls who were also on their way back to Kovno. Among them was Berl Dov Rudman, who after a few years became a member of the same "Collective" of the "Pioneer Youth" as myself, which was established in the ghetto. We joined that group and continued on our way in the direction of Kovno. At the entrance of a village, a few Lithuanian men, with white stripes on their sleeves, stopped us. Their commander had a gun and a convertible car and he smelled of alcohol. He started to investigate who we were, where we came from and where we were going. I told him that the Russians had taken my parents from their apartment and put them on a train, that we were looking for them, and that I was now on my way back to Kovno. They searched me bodily and one of his helpers found a pack of money behind my belt in the trousers, wrapped in a handkerchief. It was approximately half the amount Father had given me, the other half I kept at the bottom of my rucksack. When the commander saw this sum of money, he took my Identity card from me, telling me that I would get it back at some address in Kovno, which was, as I found out later, the Police Headquarters. After a few minutes he thought it over and decided that it would be safer for him to kill me. He put me on the back seat of his car, together with two men with shovels, one on each side of me. He himself sat at the steering wheel, but before he began to move, a young girl, apparently his sweetheart, jumped into the car and sat next to him. I tried to say something, to beg for my life. The girl talked to him and caressed him. I imagine she did not want her boyfriend to be a murderer. He stopped the car and ordered me to run to my companions, whom he had freed. At one moment I thought that he would shoot me in the back, but it was my luck that murders were as yet not so common in the first days of the war. My shoes, which I had already removed by order of the commander, were thrown after me and so I ran with my rucksack and my shoes in my hands until I reached the group. We continued to walk and on that day in the afternoon, it was Sunday, we entered Kovno. The scene we saw in the city was amazing. Many German soldiers were in the streets and

convoys of military trucks passed through. I had never seen such large trucks before and this scene clearly gave me the impression of the might and power before me.

In Kovno we parted and I walked along, my rucksack in my hand covered by my light raincoat, in order not to draw attention. I reached my room safely and was very happy to be surrounded again by friendly people. I was dirty and tired and it is difficult to describe the pleasure of sitting in a bathtub filled with warm water and of sleeping in my own bed. I had been away only five days, but it seemed to me that at least a month had passed. My friend Moshe Vald arrived safely in his room in the old city and from there he went home. He reached his family's farm and after about a month was murdered together with all the Jews in the vicinity.

The Beginning of Nazi Rule

At the beginning of July, the orders of the German Governor concerning the Jews appeared on the city's billboards. It was forbidden for them to walk on the sidewalks, only on the road itself; they had to wear yellow patches on their clothes on the left side of the chest and on the back; they had to hand over all radios and any weapons they had to the police; Jews were dismissed from all public institutions etc etc. Every few days a new decree was published, and suddenly you became an animal without any rights and in fact everybody who wanted to hurt you could do so without being punished for it. Looking back, this actually was the situation, but it took a long time for most people to become consciously aware of it.

As mentioned above, I lived on the "Green Hill" in Leliju Street. This was a quiet street, with two story houses and small gardens surrounding every house, in which mostly clerks, liberal professionals and only a few Jewish families lived. Maybe this was the reason why they were not harassed during the month and a half until August 15th, the date the Ghetto was closed. I had enough to eat during this time because I had money, and I bought food products directly from the peasants, waiting for them on the main road before they entered the city.

Later I heard that in these days the Lithuanian collaborators caught Jews in the streets and in their apartments and transported them to the Seventh Fort. Jews who returned to Kovno, having tried to escape like myself, but had gone on the main road, were also arrested and conveyed to that Fort. This was one of the nine forts built by the Tzars around Kovno, which, during the period of Independent Lithuania, were used for different purposes, such as prisons or hospitals for mental illnesses, for warehouses etc. About 10,000 Jews were brought to this fort, and kept there for many days in the burning sun without food and water, lying on the ground. Anyone who raised his head was shot. The women were kept in the cellars and at night young women were taken out, abused and shot. In a matter of a few weeks all the men were murdered, whereas the women were transported to another fort and later freed.

My second cousin, Ya'akov Gidansky and his Uncle William, who was married to Ya'akov's mother, were taken from their apartments in the main street of Kovno and brought to the Seventh Fort. After a few days, German officers came and asked for vulcanization workers or simply for workers to repair flat tires. Ya'akov, who was a Chemical Engineer and worked in a rubber factory, stood up and offered to do the work. The Germans took him with them and as a result he was rescued from this terrible place. His Uncle William refused to volunteer, as a result of which he stayed there and was shot. Ya'akov's father, William's brother, was enrolled in the German Army during World War I and died of typhus somewhere in Macedonia. His brother William later married Ya'akov's mother, Esther, who was my mother's cousin, and, of course, Barukh's too.

Ya'akov seems to be one of the few men who survived this terrible fort. He lived in Tel Aviv and at the age of 94 he passed away.

A Letter from Mother

On July 12th a Lithuanian woman brought me a letter from Mother dated the first of that month. From this letter I learned that a few weeks after the German invasion all Jewish men in Kibart from 14 years of age were taken to work at an unknown place. The women and children were evicted from their apartments and placed into the empty barracks of the Red Army. She also wrote that it is not known where the men were and that there are frightening rumors as to their destiny. The situation in the camp is very bitter and that I should not try to come to Kibart. The woman told me that a suitcase with all my things were at her house. This letter from Mother I carried with me for a long time, until my wallet was stolen including the letter. After the war I found out that the Jewish men from Kibart were taken to the gravel quarry, about 2-3 km from the town. There they were forced to excavate big pits and then they were shot on the July 7th and buried in those pits. When I got the letter from Mother I was not able to assume that Father was not alive any more, and also that the possibility of killing people without reason existed. Mother and Tekhiyah were shot in the fields of Virbalis on September 11, 1941. Memorials were erected on the mass graves. *(see Photos)*

The woman who brought me Mother's letter lived in a village not far from Kibart and for many years had been bringing butter to us from her farm. She used to tell us that her brother was a high officer in the Lithuanian Army and his family name was Vitkauskas. When the war started, he retreated with a part of that army into Russia and when he returned to Lithuania had risen to the rank of Colonel.

The tombstone on the mass graves near Kibart with the inscriptions in Yiddish and Lithuanian: "In this place were murdered by the Nazis and their local helpers the Jews of Kibart and a group of Lithuanians"

Among the victims there were the author's father and cousins Aryeh and Elyakim Leibovitz

The tombstone in memoriam of three Jewish communities:
Pilvishky, Kibart, Virbaln (Lithuania) at the cemetery in Holon-Israel.

The monument established in 1991 on the mass graves near Virbaln.

The inscriptions in Lithuanian and Yiddish on the tables says:

"Here was spilled the blood of about 10,000 Jews (Men, Women and Children), Lithuanians, war prisoners of different nationalities, who were cruelly murdered by the Nazi murderers and their helpers in July and August 1941"

Among the victims there were Mother, Tekhiya, Aunt Sarah and Tsipora.

Chapter 6: In the Kovno Ghetto
(August 15, 1941-February 1, 1944)

August 15, 1941 was the last date for the Jews of Kovno to be held in the Ghetto, which was established in the Slabodka *(Viliampole)* suburb across the river Viliya, a tributary of the river Neman. The greater part of the Ghetto was in the old Jewish quarter, famous for its "Yeshivoth." The other part was taken from Lithuanian inhabitants, who were resettled somewhere else. The Ghetto was divided into two parts by the main road to Northern Lithuania, the Big Ghetto and the Small Ghetto. These two were connected by a wooden bridge built over the road. The bridge was designed by Jewish engineers and built by Jewish carpenters from the Ghetto.

In order to settle all Jews from Kovno and from a few villages in the vicinity into the Ghetto, a Housing Commission *(Wohnungsamt)* was established, whose task it was to provide housing. Each apartment had to accomodate several families and the overcrowding was unbearable. I joined the Landau family, who had a place in the Small Ghetto. On one of those days, when many people were not yet settled, I met Ya'akov Gidansky. He invited me to come and live with his family. Since the Housing Commission jammed families who were strangers to each other into one apartment, people preferred to live together with family members or friends. So I accepted Ya'akov's invitation and moved to their apartment in the Big Ghetto. They had been allotted a two room apartment in a one story house which had been requisitioned from its Lithuanian inhabitants and been annexed to the Ghetto. Into this apartment the following were jammed: Ya'akov and his wife, her sister Clara with her husband (Milner) and their baby girl Jana, the mother of the two sisters, Ya'akov's mother Esther, his father's sister Clara Shnucal with her two sons, 16- 18 years of age and me. These people were members of one large family, but to it were added an old couple Carno, and a young man Beno Klugman, who was a refugee from Poland. His father was a journalist in Poland and he with another son were also in the Ghetto. One evening, on the eve of "Rosh Hashanah," a short time after the Ghetto was closed, as Jewish people were returning from work in town, there stood Corporal Jordan, then in charge of the Ghetto, near the Ghetto gate and he shot 10 men dead. Among them was Beno Klugman who was a nice man. He reminded me of the Italian actor Vittorio Gasman. His father and brother survived the "Holocaust" and came to Israel, where the father continued his profession as a journalist.

On August 14th, one day before the Ghetto was closed, "The Council of the Elders" *(Aeltestenrat)* published an announcement saying in effect that the Germans needed 500 intelligent and well-dressed men to put some files in order in Kovno. The next morning only about 200 men came to the Ghetto gate. As a result, the Germans and their helpers from the Lithuanian Police apprehended men directly from the streets and houses. After they had seized 534 men, they put them on trucks and transported them to the Fourth Fort, where they were shot.

The two sons of Rachel Shnucal, Ya'akov's aunt, who replied to the announcement of the "Aeltestenrat" as well Clara Milner's husband, who was seized from his apartment, were among those victims. This was part of the German method of killing the Jewish intelligentsia first. At the time, we did not know what happened to these men. The Germans spread rumors by way of their Lithuanian helpers, that these men were seen working in different places and even that some families had received letters from them, all this being a trick to misinform the public, so as to be able to perform their murderous plan quietly and without trouble. The Mother of these two sons hoped for years that they would come home one day.

On October 4th the "Small Ghetto" was liquidated, when all its inhabitants were led on foot to the Ninth Fort and shot. The hospital which had been established a short time before in the "Small Ghetto" was burned down by the Germans, including its patients and several doctors and nurses. Only people who were in possession of the special document for craftsmen (Jordanscheine) or had enough money to buy one, were allowed to cross the bridge to the "Big Ghetto." This was also one of the German practices, carried out in each Ghetto, with the aim of making Jews fight each other. I did not have such a document and I had no chance of getting one, but I had been lucky to agree to Ya'akov's offer to live with them in the "Big Ghetto." Fortunately, the Landau family had received or purchased this document and therefore moved to the "Big Ghetto."

The Great Robbery

After closing the Ghetto the Germans began to rob everything they could lay their hands on. They went from house to house in groups of three to four men, took everything they wanted, and as a measure of intimidation shot a man from time to time. This continued for several weeks, until the man in charge of the Ghetto appeared one day to announce that plunder and terror would stop if the Ghetto inhabitants themselves would hand over all the valuables they had including money, silver, gold, jewelry, musical instruments, stamp collections etc, etc. All these items were to be brought to the offices of the "Aeltestenrat" on a fixed date. This order was, as usual, accompanied with the threat, that anyone not handing over these items would be shot, together with his family. After this period of terror which had lasted for several weeks, the Jews were only too glad to hand over everything they had. On the day set for this purpose, the Germans came with several trucks, loaded them with innumerable amounts of belongings and left. This was just another German method to rob Jews of their property.

Selected sites (■) of Jewish slave labor outside the ghetto

Enterprises that used Jewish slave labor	
Airfield	Munitions Depot
Army Procurement Office	Ostland Iron Works
Army Quartering Office	Plumbing Construction
Cannery	Administration
Cement Factory	Potato Warehouse
City Water Supply	Railway Administration
Coal Transport	Office
Commercial Laundry	Railway Repair Depot
Electrical Transmission	Roofing-Felt Factory
Station	Rubber Factory
Engineering and Machine	Sawmill
Factory	Depot for Sorting of
Farming	Materials Confiscated
Foundry	from Jews
German Labor Office	Water Treatment Plant
Infirmary	Wood Chipping Factory
Lumber Yard	Wood Distribution Point
Meat-Packing Plant	

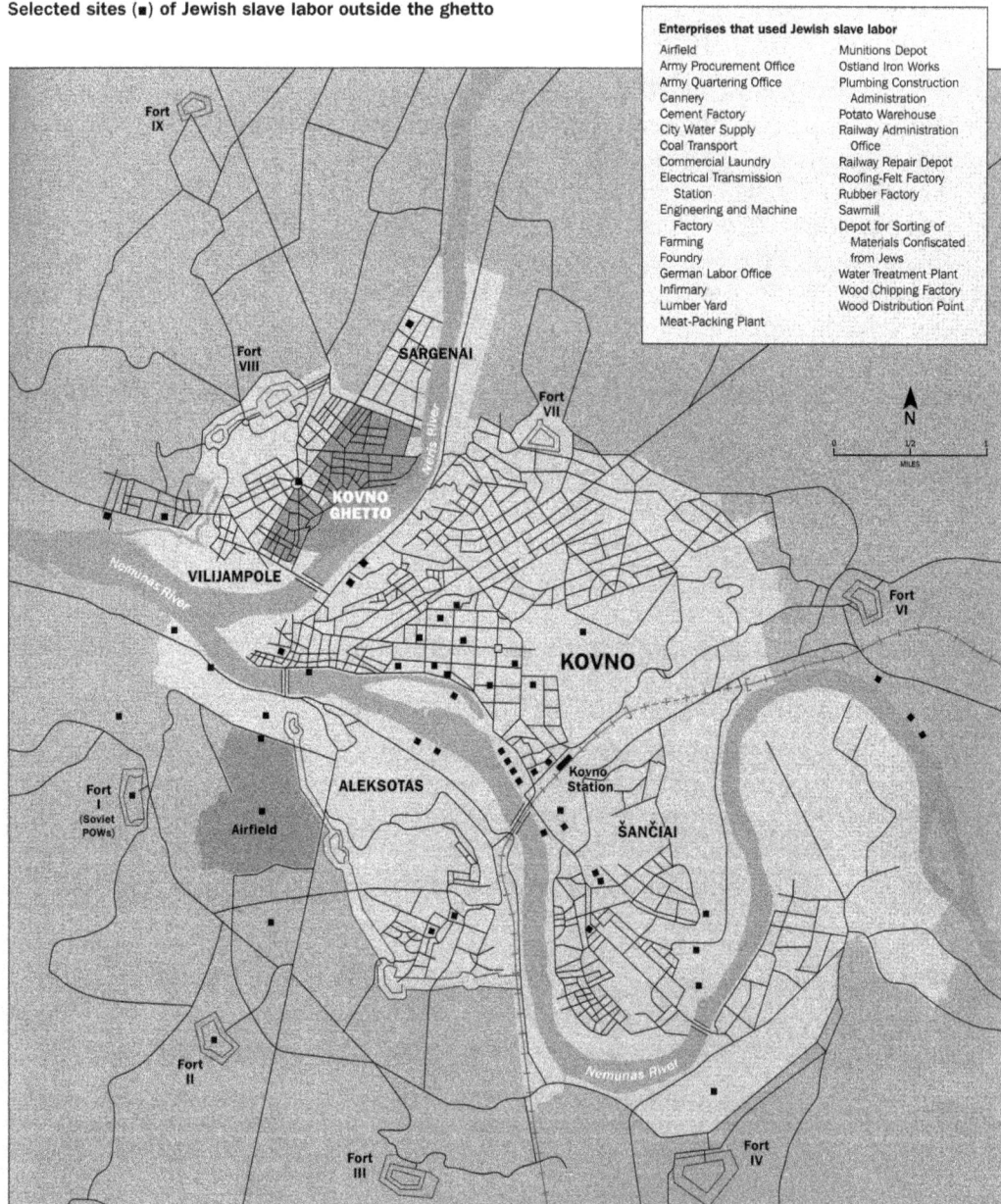

Map from the book _Hidden History of the Kovno Ghetto_
Reprinted here with the permission of the U.S. Holocaust Memorial Museum

I still had some valid Russian rubles, but because of family pressure I gave them away and so had nothing. The family I lived with also gave away everything they had, except for two items they hid in the ventilation vent in a shutter in the ceiling of the room. Through this shutter we lowered a thick golden necklace and a golden ring with a diamond, and tied it to the shutter with some cord. After the area of the Ghetto was reduced in the summer of 1942, we had to move to another apartment in Stulginskio Street NR. 6, a one story wooden house with three apartments. In our apartment, which included two small rooms and a kitchen, we were eight people: Ya'akov and his wife Sonia, Clara and her daughter Jana, the mother of the two sisters Mrs. Shapira, Ya'akov's mother and his aunt Clara, and me. I slept in a collapsible bed in the kitchen. There was running water in the house, but the conveniences were in a wooden hut in the backyard. To wash myself I had to go to the public baths in the Ghetto. After moving into the new apartment, Ya'akov and his wife decided to take the two valuable jewels for safekeeping to the Lithuanian engineer Mackevicius, who worked together with Ya'akov in the rubber factory "Guma." Ya'akov had worked in this same factory before the war as a Chemical Engineer, but now he was a forced laborer. This was a good place to work as there was also the chance of exchanging some garments for food with the Lithuanian workers in that factory. This was in contrast to the Airport *(Flugplatz)*, where Ghetto laborers worked in two shifts, 12 hours each. They were isolated from the local population and could not obtain anything worth smuggling into the Ghetto, except, occasionally, a few pieces of wood for cooking and heating.

The Work at the Airport

From mid September 1941, I worked, together with a few thousand other Jews from the Ghetto, men and women, at the "Flugplatz," where the Germans were engaged in building a big military airport. The airport was built in the suburb of Kovno Alexot (Aleksotas), near the above-mentioned building of the University. The distance between the Ghetto and the airport was about 5-6 km, some of it uphill. To get there we had to walk, accompanied by an armed guard. We had to cross the bridge on the Viliya, go through the old city, cross the bridge over the Neman and then climb up the hill to Alexot. It took 14-16 hours until we returned home, depending on the length of the queue near the gate of the Ghetto, where the Germans searched the laborers from the "Brigades" who worked in the city, for food products, since it was forbidden to bring food into the Ghetto. At the "Flugplatz" workers were usually not searched, because it was known that they had no chance of buying food.

At the airport I was forced to do work I had never done before. I carried 50 kg. sacks of cement on my back, dug channels with a shovel, carried rails on my shoulders, emptied latrines with buckets etc, etc, and all this outdoors in winter and in summer, day and night, most of the time being shouted at and beaten with a stick. The oncoming winter, with its rains and frosts, made my situation worse, because my clothes and my good shoes were very worn. The work in the field and in the ditches was sometimes in water and in mud and I got wet feet. I have to point out that I never contracted a cold or angina, something which had happened often when I used to live under normal conditions. I had no clothes, because, as stated before, I left almost everything at home in Kibart. Ya'akov's clothes were too small for me, because he was shorter and slimmer than me. Rachel Shnucal had her sons' clothes which were my size, but she did not want to give them to me, because she hoped that one day they would return home. Nevertheless I got underclothes, a sweater, socks etc. from her and from Esther. The problem was a coat.

My cousin Yitskhak Hilelson lived in the Ghetto with his lovely blond wife, her mother and their new born baby boy. To feed a baby in the Ghetto was a hard task, because there were no shops where you could buy food or anything else. The baby's mother used to leave the Ghetto with some people from a workers "Brigade" and then, after removing the yellow patch from her dress, she would leave the line and make her way into the city to get some food, specifically milk for her baby. One day the German guard of the "Brigade" saw her leaving the line and shot her dead. The baby and his grandmother were taken to their death in March 1944 in the terrible action against children and old people (Kinderaction). Yitskhak himself jumped from the train which transported the last Jews from the Kovno Ghetto to Germany in July 1944. He succeeded in coming close to his home village Sudarg and there, with the help of an old Lithuanian friend, he dug a pit in a nearby forest and lived in it for almost six months, while his friend supplied him with food. (He arrived in Israel in 1956 with his second wife, her parents and a little boy.) At the time, I went to Yitskhak and asked him if, by chance, he had an extra coat to give to me. Without any hesitation, he took a new coat from the cupboard and gave it to me. Esther sewed a balaclava for me, from woolen cloth, and also found me gloves. Thus I was able to withstand the harsh frosts and winds of winter 1941-42, when the temperature sometimes fell to minus 30 degrees Centigrade. During the 12-hour shift, we were fed once with warm soup, most of it water and a little cabbage, sometimes also potatoes.

The economic situation in the house of my relatives was relatively good. Before the war the parents of Sonia and Clara (Shapira) had owned a cosmetics store in the main street of Kovno. They were wealthy people, and brought many garments and cosmetics with them into the Ghetto. Ya'akov worked, as mentioned before, in a rubber factory, and Sonia also worked, in a "Good Brigade." Both had the opportunity to exchange items for food and to smuggle them into the Ghetto. Clara did not work, being the mother of a little girl, nor did Esther and Mrs. Shnucal, who were above the age of compulsory work. The mother of the sisters, Mrs. Shapira, was taken to her death on October 28, 1941, during the "Great Action." (See below). I remember that at some time, maybe during the relatively "Quiet Period" in the Ghetto, *(from November 1941 until the autumn of 1943),* there was even a maid in the house named Khaya, who cooked, washed and cleaned the apartment.

Going to work I always had one or two sandwiches with me, and coming back home I found some cooked food for me in a pot. I would say that I was not hungry to the extent that my life was endangered. I remember some arguments in the house, as to why only Ya'akov and Sonia had to feed me, and why Esther did not sell things for me too. In retrospect I can say that we got by somehow, when I lived with my relatives from September 1941 until December 1943. During those two years I survived thanks to their generosity and ongoing support, only a few times did I have the opportunity to exchange some things for food to bring home. Then I joined the "Collective" *(see below)* of the Zionist Pioneer Youth Movements, which was situated in two apartments in Mildos Street 7.

During the winter of 1941-42 and most of the summer of 1942 I worked on the "Flugplatz." For a short period I was attached to a brigade that worked at the baths *(Entlausung)* in the railway station of Kovno. Trains passed through the station, with soldiers who were going on leave, wounded soldiers and also forced labor, mostly women, who were apprehended throughout Russia and sent to Germany. All passing through had to wash in these baths, their clothes being put into an oven in order to kill the lice. I introduced myself as an electrician, whereupon a German gave me an iron to repair. I had no spare parts, so I connected the wires, but this functioned only for a short time and as a result I was busy with this iron for many days. Sometimes I helped to take or collect the temporary clothes which were given to the laborers for the time their clothes were in the oven. This was a good place to work in, because we were under a roof and also received a meal. I worked there for a short period only. Many people wanted to work in such a good place, but there was favoritism by, and maybe also bribery of the Jewish foreman of the brigade, who would choose the laborers, in most cases, by himself. So I went back to the "Flugplatz."

The "Great Action"

Several days before October 28, 1941, the "Aeltestenrat" published an order from the Gestapo, to the effect that all inhabitants of the Ghetto, including the old and sick, have to come on that date at 6 o'clock in the morning to the "Demokratu Square." Anybody found at home, would be shot. Rumors had spread in the Ghetto that the aim of this gathering was to divide the people into those who could contribute to the "War Effort," and others who could not work. The latter would be settled in the "Small Ghetto" and the first would get more food and better conditions. In fact, a Gestapo Officer named Rauka stood there from morning until evening, sorting the people who came before him with a stick, to the left or to the right. *(He lived in Canada until the 1980's. He was deported to Germany where he died in prison waiting for his trial).*

All the 26,000 inhabitants of the Ghetto marched slowly in front of that man and his entourage, where, with his stick, he marked those who were to go to the right, to death, and the others, who were to go to the left, to continue to suffer in the Ghetto. On that day, about 10,000 people, men, women and children, were sent to the right hand side. They spent the night in the empty "Small Ghetto," and next morning they were taken by foot to the Ninth Fort. Throughout the day we heard machine guns shooting in the Ghetto resulting in the murders of many people. The murdered were buried in big pits, which had been dug earlier by Russian war prisoners.

I had gone together with Clara who pushed a stroller, Ya'akov and Sonia and Mrs. Shapira. I had no idea of what was going on in that square. As we got near to Rauka and his gang, the Jewish Policemen, who already knew what was happening, made sure that my appearance be nice and strong. They told me to roll down the top of my coat and to take off the head and ear cover. As we approached Rauka, I heard the order "Alte rechts!" *(The old to the right)*, and soon Mrs. Shapira was torn from us and taken to the right. We did not see her again.

By evening the selection was finished. Those separated to the right were taken to the "Small Ghetto," the others were allowed to return to their homes. After standing 14 hours on their feet without drinking or eating, people returned to their apartments. Significant people who were a part of their families were torn away from them. In many houses some of the apartments were empty, because their inhabitants had been taken to their death. Esther and Clara passed the selection and returned home.

This was the darkest day in the Kovno Ghetto and was called "The Great Action." To this day and on this date, Memorial Rallies for

Lithuanian Jewry take place in Israel as well as in other places throughout the world to commemorate this horrible event so that we never forget what happened on that day so many years ago.

An analysis of the situation showed that families, in which the number of non-working people were few, passed the selection. But by evening, when the Germans realized that the required quota of those sentenced to death had not been achieved, they directed whole groups to the right, without further thought.

One day, I think it was in the winter of 1942, a friend of the Shapira family, Engineer Gerzon, turned to me and asked me if I would agree to marry Clara fictitiously. She thought, according to the rumors that circulated in the Ghetto, that her situation, no husband and having a little girl, would be safer if she would have a young strong husband. I agreed without too much thought. We went to the "Aeltestenrat" and there this was recorded, without any ritual. Looking back now, it is clear that it did not make any difference. My life did not change after the "Wedding," but I felt a little better, having repaid a favor with a favor.

The "Action" for Riga

On February 6, 1942 the Germans issued an order, demanding that 500 people be sent to work in Riga, the capital of Latvia. After the previous "Actions" and killings, the Ghetto inhabitants did not believe that people were going to be sent for work purposes and not to their death. The "Aeltestenrat" and the Ghetto Police did not manage to gather the required number of people fast enough, so the Germans started to take people straight from their houses, offices, workshops etc. On that day I happened to be with the Landau family, who lived near "Demokratu" Square. When we saw what was going on in the square, where those caught were being contained, Mr. Landau, his son and I hid in a cavity under the floor. We lay there all day long and Mrs. Landau passed some food to us, informing us about events in the square. The people who were caught on that day were actually sent to Riga for the purpose of work, but because they were taken without thought or consideration, many families were left without their breadwinner.

My Outings into the City

I have already described the friendship between the Landau and Dushauskas families, which started when the two men were in jail. After the Ghetto was closed, the Lithuanian family brought some food for the Landaus, but when the situation became dangerous they stopped. Nevertheless, since their relationship continued, the Landau family decided to send their son David to live with the Dushauskas, who lived in a two story house without any neighbors on the "Green Hill." He was 15 years old, with blond hair and blue eyes, just like the only Dushauskas son. One day Mr. Landau asked me if I would be ready to hand over a $20 golden coin to Mr. Dushauskas, and despite the danger of doing so, I agreed. I was well dressed, with the coat I received from my cousin and my appearance could be taken as that of a "Goy." I left the Ghetto with a "Flugplatz" brigade, and while walking in the old city, took off the yellow patches from my coat, left the group, and made my way to the Dushauskas house. There they warmly welcomed me and I handed over the coin which I had hidden in my shoe. I talked with David, I had lunch with them, soup with much bread and a main course, and waited until the time when the brigades were about to go home. Then I went to one of the streets where they passed and joined one of them. I joined a line of marchers and attached the yellow patches to my coat with a safety pin. I carried out this routine once or twice more. Once, when waiting in a lane for a brigade to come, I saw a young woman, who seemingly was also Jewish, also waiting for a brigade. I waited for some time, but no brigade arrived. Meanwhile Lithuanian children began to shout after us "*Zydas*" *(Jew)*. I understood that something had gone wrong and I had come too late. It was Sunday and only a few brigades were working. Maybe they had been sent home before their regular time. I had no choice, returned to Dushauskas and spent the night and the next day with them, until I met another brigade and came home with it.

If I ask myself now, why I did it, knowing that I could endanger myself as well as my hosts, the answer is, that what persuaded me to take this action was the tremendous contrast between spending a day in a warm house and having a good meal as compared to working at the "Flugplatz." Furthermore, Mr. Landau gave me some money for the favor I had done him. Previously, I had been penniless, but now having some money I could buy a beigel or a roll sometimes, these were baked illegally in the Ghetto. Later I got information that the Dushauskas had hidden more Jews and after they were caught or suspected, Mr. Dushauskas was sent to a concentration camp situated about 30 km. from Kovno. As a former high official he had many friends, who freed him from that camp after a short time. I will tell more about him in subsequent pages.

The Palemon Camp

One night in autumn 1942 I found myself in the ghetto jail, together with tens of young men who had been taken there from their beds. From there we were sent to Palemon, a railway station not far from Kovno, where the German semimilitary engineering company "Organization Todt" was building big storehouses. Billeted in a camp, we were put up in huts, where Soviet war prisoners had lived before. These were full of lice. After one night there I was also full of them. The commander of the camp was a middle aged German who was always shouting and beating people and once shot a young man to death, who apparently was ill and did not get up for work in the morning. The work was not hard and among the guards there were a few who demonstrated a humane attitude towards us. The guards included Italians, one Frenchman and several Bosnians from Yugoslavia. But the conditions and the food were very bad. There was some contact with the Ghetto and sometimes we received food parcels from our families and, if I am not mistaken, also letters. Once, I remember, I received a two kg. loaf of bread from Ya'akov, which was wet and heavy. After work I sat down and ate it all at once. In that camp I first met Khayim Gechtel (later Galin). We became friends and have remained so to this day. *(passed away a few years ago).*

I stayed in this camp about one to two months. It is difficult to reconstruct the time table. I remember only, that one day a group of us were taken to the bathhouse in the Ghetto, where Jewish doctors checked our health. When a doctor lifted my arm and looked at my armpit, he called more doctors and sisters to see the horror. After taking a bath and getting treatment against lice, I did not return to Palemon. It turned out that Ya'akov had made efforts in the Employment Office of the Ghetto to bring me back from there.

In the Ghetto Police and in the Underground

After the unpleasant experience in Palemon I worked in different places. One day in the spring of 1943 I was attached to a brigade, which worked in the port on the river Neman. We had to pull out logs from the water and load them onto trolleys, which transported them to a nearby sawmill. It was hard work, because the logs were very heavy, as they were still covered with ice. In my group, there were two young men I did not know at the time. One was Josi Melamed, now a member of Kibbutz Lehavoth HaBashan *(passed away several months ago)*, the other was Leo Simon *(was caught by the Gestapo on his way to Agustova and was killed)*. Carrying logs, we talked about different subjects, and after Leo heard that I was a member of

"HaShomer-HaTsair," he invited me to come to a certain address in the Ghetto for a meeting of members of that movement. This was the address of Ali Rauzuk, who was the head of the movement in the Ghetto. So I joined the Socialist Zionist Underground in the Ghetto, which already had contact with the Communists. Together they planned resistance actions against the Germans in the Ghetto or how to join the Partisans.

This accidental meeting at the port with Leo Simon was crucial for me. I can say now, in retrospect, that it changed the direction of my life and maybe that thanks to this I survived.

At this time it was announced in the Ghetto, that the number of Ghetto policemen would be increased and applicants were needed. According to experience so far, it seemed that policemen and their families were safer from maltreatment, so my relatives influenced me to try to enroll in the police. It was no doubt more convenient and more pleasant to stay in the Ghetto, instead of working hard outside and mostly with much abuse. I also did not see, according to the functions the police fulfilled in the Ghetto, anything amoral or negative in being a policeman. Only after the war did I become aware of the very negative functions of the Jewish police in many Ghettos.

In brief, I applied and was accepted into the police, in spite of the fact that I did not think I stood a chance. Later I got to know that there were two factors that helped me get into the police: One was the intercession of my relatives who knew the police commanders, and the second was the Underground which was interested in having some of its members be a part of the police. Several police officers were connected with the Underground, like Yehuda Zupovitz and Ika Grinberg, also the commander of the Ghetto police Moshe Levin was informed about the Underground and helped it as much as he could. I got a service cap with the police emblem and an armband on which was written in German "Ghetto Polizei." I was a policeman for about half a year until I was fired, because the Ghetto quarters were reduced by a third, and so were the number of police.

The function of the Ghetto Police was to keep public order. The policemen had no guns, not even sticks. Their authority came only from the cap and the armband, but this worked. During the short time I was in the Police, my main task was to look for people who did not report for work, or to collect people, whose names appeared on previously prepared lists, to be sent to work to different places outside of the Ghetto. Sometimes, at night, I patrolled a certain section along the Ghetto fence, while on the outer side of the fence there was a Lithuanian guard armed with a gun. On these patrols I was sometimes witness to the smuggling of food products into the Ghetto by Jewish traders. They bribed the Lithuanian guard and

From left: chief of the Ghetto Police-Moshe Levin, deputy-Yehuda Zupovitz, gate guard-Tankhum Arnshtam

Labor brigades returning from work standing before the Ghetto gate.

-Yehushua Grinberg deputy chief of the police

JÜDISCHE
GHETTO-POLIZEI
11

The armband of the Ghetto police

AUSWEIS

FÜR JÜDISCHE HANDWERKER

OIZ JORDAN

The "Jordan Certificate" for Jewish artisans

The bridge on Paneriu Street which connected the Great and the Small Ghettos (painted by Esther Lurie)

threw the sacks with the products over the barbed wire fence. I also received some money from them and in the morning, after the patrol, I bought myself a warm roll straight from the oven. During these days it was possible to buy, for high prices, almost anything in the way of food products in the camouflaged stores of the Ghetto. In Kovno too all the food was rationed and the black market flourished. In the Ghetto the black market was illegal, according to the German authorities, but, of course, not for the Jews, in spite of the fact that only a few had enough money to benefit from these shops.

At nights there was a curfew in the Ghetto, but as a policeman I was able to go out at night into the streets, and also to take other people with me. The commanders of the Underground used this privilege of mine and occasionally asked me to transport people from one address to another, at night. I did not know these people and after bringing the man or the woman to a certain address, I was asked to wait outside, and when he or she finished his or her business I had to bring them to another address or home. These were the people of the joint headquarters of the Underground.

I also had to inform Ali Rauzuk, the head of the "HaShomer-HaTsair"organization in the Ghetto about everything I heard in the Police, which would alert the members of the Underground to any possibility of trouble.

The Big Workshops of the Ghetto

One day I was asked by the Underground to escort Mira Buz (she passed away a few years ago in Lehavoth HaBashan) and her friend to the big workshops of the Ghetto, with the aim of stealing some equipment for members of the Underground who were to join the Partisans in the woods of Augustova. *(To this case I refer later on)*

The big workshops of the Ghetto worked mainly for the German Army. There were, among others, workshops for sewers, shoemakers, locksmiths, carpenters, hatters, furriers, brush and basket makers etc. 3,000-4,000 Ghetto Jews worked there, in two shifts. Most of them were craftsmen, others had benefited from favoritism. This was a convenient place of work, because it was situated inside the Ghetto borders and there were no German supervisors. The workshops were surrounded by a high concrete wall and the entrance was through a guarded gate.

Mira and her friend's plan were to climb over the fence, get into the workshops and take the needed equipment, mainly clothes and boots. For this purpose they had brought a few empty sacks with them. My job was to warn them if anybody was approaching. It so happened, that two officers of the Ghetto Police came to the place from an unexpected direction and met Mira with her friend. The policemen did not see me, because it was dark, and I ran away. They were both taken to the Police station and interrogated about their activities in that place and at night. They answered that it was a romantic encounter. And why the sacks they were then asked. To lie on was the answer. They were soon released, without further fuss.

Several months later, when organized armed youth groups started to leave the Ghetto for the Partisans in the woods in order to fight against the Nazis, they were equipped, with the knowledge of the workshop directors, with German uniforms, boots, belts etc.

The "Action" for Estonia

At the end of October 1943 the Germans ordered the collection of 3,000 men and women for a transport to a labor camp in the village of Ezereciai in Lithuania, where they would work in the woods and dig peat. This village was not far from Kovno, and at first there was no objection among those people who were informed that they were on the lists to be sent to Ezereciai, and that they had to be ready. It was known in the Ghetto that the Germans intended to disperse most of the Ghetto population into labor camps, so the candidates for Ezereciai accepted the judgment. But due to some signs, doubts began to infiltrate into the Ghetto, as to whether these people were really going to Ezereciai or God knew where. So people who appeared on these lists began to run from one place to another, trying not to be found in their apartments. Then the Germans brought a big group of Russians and Ukrainians from the Vlasov Army (*Gen. Vlasov-collaborator with the Nazis*) into the Ghetto. They took people from their houses without any consideration, rampaging at the same time.

This was in the afternoon of October 26th. I was still a policeman and had gone to my apartment, when I saw a Ukrainian taking Sonia, Ya'akov's wife. Ya'akov himself jumped out of a window when the Ukrainians broke into the house, but they managed to catch his wife. I went to the Ukrainian, told him that she was my wife and that he should release her. He complied and she returned home.

Later it became known that on that day 2,700 people, men, women and children, were taken from the Ghetto and sent to Estonia, not to Ezereciai. Before they were loaded into the wagons, the old and the children were separated from the others and sent to Auschwitz to their death. Among those who were sent to Estonia only a few survived. With the German retreat from Estonia in July 1944, they sent most of the population of the labor camps to the concentration camps in Germany and the others were shot.

About ten days after the "Estonia Action" it became known, that in the Shavl Ghetto, one of three in Lithuania (together with Kovno and Vilna) which still existed then, an "Action" as the Germans called it, had taken place against children under the age of 12 and against people above the age of 55, as well as against the sick and the invalids. It was clear that all these people had been sent to their death. There was turmoil in the Ghetto, because it was evident that what happened in Shavl would happen in Kovno too. The problem was how to save the children. One possibility was to hand over children to Lithuanian families, who were prepared, for various reasons, to look after Jewish children. It was a complicated and dangerous operation to transfer a small child, who did not speak Lithuanian, to a strange family. The Jews of the Ghetto were not free to go to the city in order to look for a family who would be prepared to keep a little child or to take a child out from the Ghetto, which was also not easy. Much money was needed to pay a Lithuanian family for keeping a child, and by this time most of the Ghetto Jews had no money. Sometimes it happened that a Lithuanian family took a child and also money, but returned the child after a short time, making true or false excuses as to why the child needed to be returned.

In Kovno Ghetto the "Action" against children and old people took place on March 27th and March 28, 1944. On that day the Jewish policemen were taken to the Ninth Fort where they were asked by the Gestapo to reveal the places were "Malinas" *(Bunkers)* had been built in the Ghetto. On that day 40 policemen were shot, among them the Chief of the Police Mosheh Levin and his deputies Ika Grinberg and Yehudah Zupovitz.

Jana's Story

Jana was, as mentioned before, the little daughter of Clara Milner, Sonia's sister and was by now three years old. When fear for the children's fate became real, the family decided to hand over the girl to a Lithuanian family named Gvildys, who lived in Kovno. The Shapiras had lived in the Gvildys' house for many years and they had a good relationship.

After it was agreed between the families to hand over the girl, there was still the problem of getting her out of the Ghetto. It was decided to do this in the evening, at a time when there usually was much pressure and disorder near the Ghetto gate. It was necessary to anesthetize the girl, to put her into a specially prepared rucksack and I, the policeman, had to get her out through the gate and give her to a woman who was waiting at the corner of a street not far from the gate. After a few attempts of anesthesia using pills failed, as the girl did not fall asleep, Dr. Gurevitz (passed away several years ago in Israel) was brought in, and the girl was given an injection. Thereupon I carried the girl out of the Ghetto and handed her over to the Lithuanian woman. All this was performed with the help of the Jewish "Gate Guard" (Tor Wache). When the Ghetto was liquidated in July 1944, Sonia, Clara, Esther Gidansky and Clara Shnukal were sent to the Stutthof concentration camp, where they all perished. Ya'akov was sent to Dachau and survived, this time also thanks to his knowledge of repairing automobile tubes and tires. After being freed from Dachau, Ya'akov decided to go back to Kovno, hoping against all odds to find his wife there. Arriving in Kovno, he went to the Gvildys, who invited him to stay with them until he could get his life back into some reasonable order.

During the two years that Jana lived with the Gvildys, the sister of Mrs. Gvildys, who was single and not young, had grown very close to Jana and refused to give her back to her Uncle, who, in the situation he found himself in at this time, was not capable of taking care of her. So the girl remained with this woman, who adopted her as her daughter. But Jana knew that Ya'akov was her Uncle and that Miss Gvildys was not her real Mother. Relations between Ya'akov and Jana's "Mother" became cooler after Jana started to ask questions about Clara.

Meanwhile the years passed by, the girl grew up, finished high school and started to study medicine at the university. During all these years there was some contact between Jana and Ya'akov, and when Jana completed her studies, she called Ya'akov and asked if he was prepared to help her. She knew a Lithuanian boy and wanted to marry him, but her "Mother" was against the marriage. Ya'akov told her that it would not be fair of him to oppose her "Mother," however if the boy were Jewish, the situation would be different. Jana married that boy, despite her "Mother's" objection. She specialized in "Children's Medicine" and moved with her husband to Mariampol. A few years later her husband left her and her "Mother" passed away. She did not have any children. She submitted an application to go to Israel, after Ya'akov sent her the needed documents. The Soviet authorities rejected her application and she committed suicide at the age of 38. This is the tragic story of a Jewish girl, who grew up among the Lithuanians, and in whose destiny I played a small part.

On November 1, 1943 the Ghetto was turned into a Concentration Camp (K.Z. Kauen) under the authority of the S.S. The commander of the camp was an S.S. officer named Goecke, who announced his plan to divide the Ghetto into labor camps, most of them in the vicinity of Kovno. In the Ghetto itself only the big workshops and the service staff remained.

The "Collective"

The Underground was interested in its members being concentrated in one place and not scattered among the different labor camps (Kasernierung). As mentioned above, I was dismissed from the police in December 1943, and until I left for the Partisans on February 1, 1944, I did not work at all.

All that was happening in the Ghetto concerning the "Kasernierung" did not touch us. We had been selected by the Partisans, and waited for our departure to the woods. At this time I left my place in Ya'akov's apartment and moved to the "Collective" for members of "HaShomer-HaTsair" and "HeKhalutz," located in two attached apartments of two rooms each in Mildos Street 7. The Underground, coordinating with the Ghetto authorities, made sure that the members of the "Collective" would not appear in the lists of people to be sent to one of the labor camps, and also helped us to get food.

After the "Action for Estonia," people realized that anyone who had a place to hide had not been caught. As a result, people started to construct "Malina's." These were bunkers, constructed beneath the houses, with hidden entrances. Every "Malina" had to have a vent, conveniences, also water and food for a few weeks. In places where the groundwater level was not too low, they dug wells. In other places a supply of water was prepared in various containers. It was necessary to connect up to the electricity grid. At Mildos St. 7 we also started to construct a "Malina" underneath the house. The idea was to prepare a hiding place for the members, mainly for the girls, in case of an emergency situation and also for a longer stay, if and when the Red Army approached Kovno. At this time we already were in contact with the Partisans in the Rudniki woods and our comrade Shemuel Mordkovsky even reached their headquarters and returned to the Ghetto, having been given a task. He told us that the Partisan officials had no interest in receiving girls, so we thought that the "Malina" would be a reasonable solution for those who could not join the Partisans.

The construction of the "Malina" was performed mainly at night. We had to take out big quantities of sand by using buckets, and dispose of it in such a manner so as not to arouse suspicion. It was also necessary to build supports for the ceiling and the walls, so that the apartment above would not collapse into it. During the time I was in the "Collective," approximately one month, January 1944, we worked on building the "Malina" with great energy. There were then about 25 members in the "Collective," men and women, but many friends came to visit the place and some of them even helped build the "Malina."

CHAPTER 7: Among the Partisans and in the Army (February 1, 1944- August, 1944)

The Journey to Augustova

The idea of establishing a Partisan base in the woods of Augustova arose during a meeting between Chaim Yelin, the young Yiddish writer, and the head of the Communist Underground in the Ghetto and G. Ziman, the commander of the Lithuanian Partisan base. The region of Augustova was situated about 160 kilometers (100 miles) south of Kovno, on the border between Poland and Prussia.

G. Ziman was a teacher in a Jewish High School in Kovno and a graduate of the Hebrew High School in Mariampol. Like many others, he was parachuted by the Partisan Movement Headquarters in Moscow into Lithuania, with the aim of establishing a partisan movement and a Communist Underground in Lithuania.

He was given an Underground name, Jurgis, a typical Lithuanian name. Among the parachutists there were many Jewish boys and girls, who managed to escape to Russia during the first days of the war, and who volunteered for the job. Most of them were killed on encountering Germans or as a result of Lithuanian informers. The headquarters of the Lithuanian Partisans was established in the woods of Rudniki. It was a large wooded area with swamps southeast of Vilna; about 2,400 square km. in size, and its shape was rectangular, 40 km. wide by 60 km. long. Its northern edge was about 15 km. from Vilna and its eastern end reached Belorussia.

Establishing a Partisan base in the woods of Augustova by the Underground of the Ghetto may have been correct politically, but absolutely wrong from a practical point of view. Politically it was right to show Moscow that there was a Lithuanian Partisan movement in all regions of the state, but practically it was a big failure and caused several tens of victims from the best youths of the Ghetto. The first group that went to Augustova numbered 20 men and after marching about 25 km. from Kovno they did not find the right way and the group dispersed. Three men of the group were caught by the Gestapo and were returned to the Ghetto. The others returned to the Ghetto without being caught. The second group, numbering also about 20 men, collided with Lithuanian guards, some 20 km. from Kovno. Two men were killed and the rest were taken to a prison. After an investigation accompanied by blows, some of them were returned to the Ghetto, whereas six men were taken to the above-mentioned Ninth Fort. In this fort about 70,000 people were murdered, most of them Jews from Kovno, as well as Jews from Austria, Germany, Czechoslovakia and France also Jewish war prisoners from the Red Army. In the fort, the six Underground members found more members who had been caught on the roads, also war prisoners, mostly Jewish officers and a few Lithuanians, altogether about 60 people. It was their job to remove all the corpses from the mass graves and burn them, big heaps of 300 corpses each. It was November 1943 and the German victory was becoming uncertain, so they tried to cover their crimes by covering up traces of the horrors they had committed. Burning the murdered began at many mass graves at the same time, more or less. I have no wish to recall here the adventures and horrors the prisoners of the Ninth Fort went through, but it is important to mention that during the night of Christmas 1943 all the prisoners escaped from this fort. Nineteen of them infiltrated into the Ghetto, which was only 4 km. away from the fort, most of the rest were caught by the Germans. In the Ghetto they were hidden with the support of the Ghetto Authorities and the police, and after a few weeks 11 of them joined the Partisans. Five of them live in Israel and every year on December 24th they celebrate their "second birthday" together. (Two of them passed away already).

About 100 people made their way to Augustova, 40 of them were caught by the Gestapo. Six of the finest youngsters of "HaShomer HaTsair" perished in this pitiful expedition, among them Leo Simon, who had introduced me to the Underground. The main reason for their failure was the non-observance of rules of how to move in enemy territory. Where most of the population is hostile, one cannot walk in broad daylight without being caught. Another reason for the failure was the absence of up-to-date maps. Only the group leader had a hand drawn map, whereas the others had to learn the course of by heart, such as: "After 3 km. there is a channel, and then you turn to the right and go to a grove etc, etc." After a short time the youngsters realized that the maps were old, they found neither the channel nor the grove. The moment someone discovered the group, they panicked and lost their way. Only two men, Nekhemyah Endlin and Shemuel Mordkovski, reached the woods of Augustova and returned safely to the Ghetto. There they found no trace of parachutists or partisans, who were supposed to be there. The conclusion drawn from this unfortunate expedition was that it was practically impossible for the people of the Ghetto to establish a partisan base in those woods, because they did not have enough arms or enough experience in partisan fighting.

In those days I was still in the police, but as a member of the Underground I belonged to a cell of three who, among other things, studied the paths which lead to Augustova by heart. If I had been asked to participate in this expedition, I would no doubt have accepted. Fortunately I was not asked to do so, because I was needed in the Underground as a policeman. The expedition to Augustova was a disgraceful failure causing many victims, and its initiators were later rightly accused of a lack of responsibility. Looking back, this adventure showed the determination of the Ghetto youth not to sit still with folded arms, but to find any way to break out through the fences.

The Departure to the Woods

As mentioned before, there was contact at this time with the Partisan base in the woods of Rudniki and also with the Communist Underground in Kovno. The distance between Kovno and the Partisan base was about 150 km. and it was clear that big groups could not traverse this distance without being caught. After much effort, Khayim Yelin, the head of the Underground in the Ghetto, found a Lithuanian driver, who had been a member of the Comsomol *(the Communist Youth Organization),* and was employed by the German Security Police in Kovno. This driver agreed, mainly because of the payment he received and also perhaps being willing to help, to risk the trip on the truck of the German Police, from the Ghetto to near the woods of Rudniki. The first group, consisting of 17 people, went to the Partisans on this truck as a Labor Brigade, leaving after several delays, on December 14, 1943. This operation, including the financing of the truck, was carried out with the help of the Ghetto Authorities and in particular with the help of the police and the men of the Labor Office *(Arbeitsamt),* who, together with the Germans, checked the outgoing and incoming Labor Brigades.

Five more groups used this same method, each of about 20 people. The fifth group included the fugitives from the Ninth Fort. All these groups arrived safely at the Partisan base, after passing the dense and dangerous region of Central Lithuania by truck. On January 11, 1944 five Partisans, four men and one woman, returned to the Ghetto with instructions from headquarters, which included, among others, the task of transferring more groups from the Ghetto to the base. Among the four men was our above-mentioned friend Shemuel Mordkovsky. For many hours we sat with him in the flat of the "Collective," listening to his stories about sabotage and reprisal operations of the Partisans and about life in the woods. He did not resolve our immediate problems, the main one being the shortage of arms. Pistols were not considered practical for fighting. A pistol could be useful for committing suicide when you were in danger of being caught by the enemy. What we needed were rifles, machine guns, grenades etc. It was also important that every Partisan be familiar with his gun, because in the base there was no time for training.

Another problem was the base commanders' negative attitude to accepting girls. He also told us about the anti-Jewish attitudes of Russian and Ukrainian Partisans.

The fifth group, among them the fort fugitives, was not welcomed by the Regiments Commissar Davidov, because its arms were poor. The refrain: "Why did you come here? To hide and survive?" was often heard from him, while he himself, an escaped war prisoner, did not participate in any fighting operation and was practically an anti-Semite.

The sixth group started to organize in the middle of January 1944. The Zionist Socialist Youth was allotted seven places in this group and I was one of them. It is worth pointing out, that among the six, seven boys and the one girl, no one had any family left in the Ghetto, apart from her. Only she had left her mother in the Ghetto. For anyone who lived with his family, it was not so easy to abandon them and to escape. But among the boys there were a few who left their girlfriends behind in the Ghetto. During the period of the Underground and the Collective I developed a friendship with Shulamith Sukenik. She was a lovely girl, with black hair and brown eyes, a little younger than me, but this friendship continued only for a short time. She remained in the Ghetto and later was taken to Stutthof, where she perished. Before I left the Ghetto, she gave me her photograph which I carried with me on all the adventures I went through. In Israel her cousin Peninah Sukenik-Gofer asked me for that photo, and I gave it to her.

Among the seven, one was killed as a soldier of the Red Army, one was killed fighting with the Partisans and the other five survived and live in Israel: Gita Pogir-Tur Zion in Kibbutz Reshafim, Grisha Shefer in Kibbutz Eilon, Khayim Galin and Barukh Grodnik-Gofer in Kiryath Bialik and myself.

We received the needed equipment from the Big Ghetto Workshops, illegally, of course, but with the approval of the officials in charge. This equipment included German uniforms, boots, warm underwear, coats etc. The girls in the Collective shortened the coats, knitted caps and gloves for their outgoing friends. We received some rifle training from the Deputy Chief of the Ghetto Police, Yehudah Zupovitz. It was the first time I had held a rifle in my hands and I learned how to insert a bullet into the barrel. This was the only training we had.

It was determined that our guides to the woods would be three Partisans who had recently returned to the Ghetto. The commander would be Nekhemyah Endlin, a clever man with a very good sense of orientation. He also knew how to escape from dangerous situations.

He had made that trip several times already. He came to Israel in the 1970's, published his memoirs and passed away after a few years. The second guide would be Barukh Lopiansky *(killed later in Partisan fighting)* and the third Zunia Shtrom *(came to Israel in the 1970's, died several years ago)*.

Farewell from the Ghetto

The last Sabbath eve, before leaving the Ghetto, we organized a farewell party in the Collective, in which the members of the Collective and a limited number of invited guests participated. Seated at set tables with tea and candies "Made in the Ghetto," which were famous also outside of the Ghetto, we recalled different experiences from the Movement, the camps etc. Yerakhmiel Voskoboinik had a collection of all the songs we used to sing in the Movement and we sang them on this evening from A to Z. Ali Rauzuk made a speech on behalf of the Movement and we heard many encouraging words. We reminiscenced about our distant Jewish history: the Maccabeans, Bar-Kokhva; up to the more recent past: the Movement; to the immediate and hard present: Ghetto, slavery, despair, and we spoke loudly about our thoughts of the future: revenge, liberation, Eretz-Yisrael. The climax of this party was when, with customary ceremony, a red flag was brought in and the seven people who would be leaving, swore the oath of a "Shomer." Indeed, an unforgettable experience.

Now we were ready for departure. With warm kisses we said good-bye to all friends and one by one went to the meeting point, a half ruined building. There we received our final instructions. Homemade compasses were given to the commanders. We packed the six rifles we received into cotton blankets and put them into sacks, which we tied with rope to make them look like bags of bedding. The belts with the bullets we wore under our coats. We stood about 100 meters from the gate, on the corner of Varniu and Paneriu streets, and waited for the truck, which in the end, did not arrive on that afternoon. The same happened a few days later. Only the third time, on February 1, 1944, did we leave. Meanwhile several changes occurred: some people gave up their places for others and also the quantity of our arms increased. The seven of our group were firm and did not give up, as we knew that this was the right way and that there was no alternative. We received a Russian machine gun with a cartridge of 72 bullets, packed just like the rifles.

Eventually the great moment arrived. A truck, covered on all sides with tarpaulin, stopped at the gate and then we heard the call "Babtai" when we appeared. Babtai was a small town not far from

Kovno, where a labor brigade from the Ghetto was working and its people came to the Ghetto every few weeks. We approached the gate quickly, five persons in a line as usual. The Jewish Arbeitsamt man in charge of that gate gave a clean piece of paper to one man of the group, i.e. an "Exit Permission" and the SS man shouted "Thirty men, all right." Running fast, we passed the gate and jumped onto the truck. Nekhemyah Endlin sat in the driver's cabin, the rear tarpaulin went down and the truck moved.

We were travelling through the streets of Kovno, which most of us remembered nostalgically. Here was the turn to Jurbarko Street, here the bridge over the Viliya and here Jonavos Street in the old part of Kovno. Suddenly the truck stopped. A Jewish boy and a Jewish girl lifted a sack onto the truck, which contained 18 rifles, some grenades, a few pistols and also medical equipment. All this stuff had been hidden with a Lithuanian member of the Underground. Now we were in the middle of the city. It was dark and crowded in the truck and it stopped again. We stopped breathing and could hear our hearts beating. Nobody knew what was happening. Soon, maybe, the tarpaulin would be lifted and curious eyes would look inside. It was quiet outside, but minutes seemed like hours. Later we understood that the driver had stopped at his house to bring some food for the journey. We continued and soon were outside the city. The most dangerous area was behind us. In the truck we heard the order: "Get the arms." Everybody rushed to grab his rifle and bullets. Then we were ordered: "Load the rifles." I still wonder how it came about that there was no disaster during the crush in the truck that night. Four men: Grisha Shefer, Yehudah Eidelman, Mosheh Raikhman and me were dressed in German uniforms. We fastened the belts with their imprint of the swastika and the words "Gott mit Uns" (God is with us), and sat at the back of the truck outside the tarpaulin, rifles in our hands. To any passerby this looked like a regular German Security Police truck, since its license plate was original and also the four "Policemen," two of them officers, looked very real. The people in the truck were ordered to remove the yellow patches from their back and chest, and to put them into their pockets. Now the commander said: "From this moment, comrades, you are Partisans. If somebody should try to stop us, we open fire." We felt, indeed, at this moment, that a new era had begun in our lives. We passed the town Jesnas and turned from the main road into a second grade road towards the small town of Butrimantz (Butrimonys). Ten km. beyond the town we jumped off the truck, from where we had to march another 40 km. The driver was very surprised to see us so well armed, as previous groups that he had driven were armed only with pistols.

The first peasant we met was ordered to harness a horse to a cart and onto it we loaded the heavy rucksacks we had carried with us. They were heavy because of the various types of equipment we were taking to headquarters. We ourselves went by foot. In the morning we chose a desolate farm and there we spent the day, continuing on our way in the evening. Occasionally we entrusted peasants to harness horses and carts to carry our equipment for some distance. Eventually we came near the Kovno-Grodno railway line. A peasant from nearby was our guide. Here I have to explain, that the Germans guarded the railways very well in that region, because of sabotage actions by Partisans. Along hundreds and thousands of kilometers of rail tracks, which were the main supply routes for their army, they erected mined barbed wire fences, used patrols with dogs etc. To cross a railway line was a very dangerous operation. As we crossed, by running over the tracks, we heard shots and saw rockets in the sky, but we arrived safely on the other side and at dawn we entered the Rudniki woods.

The first Partisan who saw us nearly alarmed his regiment, because four of us still wore German uniforms. We arrived in the village of Inklariskis, inside the forest. There we rested all day and the next morning continued our march. This time the Commissar of our future regiment was our guide. In Inklariskis we met a young blond Partisan, who looked like a "Goy," armed with a submachine gun. After a few minutes we realized that he was a Jewish boy from Vilna, who belonged to a nearby Partisan regiment. His name was Barukh Shub and ever since that time we have been good friends. We reached our base in the middle of the night and after registration became real Partisans in a regiment named "Death to the German Invaders." After our arrival, the Commissar searched our belongings and confiscated some items. In an earlier group he had confiscated a watch from a woman and a little pistol from a man who received it as a present in the Ghetto. This incident caused bad feelings among the Jewish Partisans, because it looked like abuse and discrimination against them. The truth was that the Russian runaway war prisoners had nothing which could be taken from them, but the abuse was there and anger mounted after the Commissar gave the confiscated watch to one of the non-Jewish patrols. After intense protests, the woman, who was a Partisan's widow who fell in battle, received her watch back.

A month later, on March 3, 1944, the seventh group of thirty men and women arrived safely at our regiment. The group traveled by the same truck and was well armed. The guides were the above-mentioned Nekhemyah Endlin, who meanwhile had returned to the Ghetto and Yisrael Goldblat, who came back from the Partisan base *(he immigrated to Israel in the 1970's.)* My friends Dov Levin and Tsevi

Braun-Bar-On *(later both professors at the Hebrew University in Jerusalem. Tsevi died several years ago)* were in this group. Dov brought me some small things sent by Shulamith, of which I remember only the saccharin and a pill.

At the end of the same month, the eighth group left the Ghetto and arrived safely in the woods. During the first part of April, when Khayim Yelin, the commander of the Ghetto Underground, was in Kovno looking for transportation for another group of 30 well armed people, he was discovered and while being pursued, shot a few Germans and Lithuanians. Badly wounded, he was caught and brought to the Gestapo, where he was questioned at length and severely tortured, but he did not give his comrades of the Underground away. This man died tragically, and it is likely thanks to him that many youths of the Ghetto survived the Holocaust.

After the death of Khayim Yelin, his friends found a driver who agreed, in return for a large sum of money, to drive another group to the woods. In the middle of April a group of 12 men left the Ghetto by truck. Near the bridge over the Viliya the driver stopped, saying that there was something wrong with the engine. At this moment shots started from all directions and all, including the driver, were killed. Only four men managed to escape and return to the Ghetto. This was the end of organized departures from the Ghetto to the woods. Only individuals arrived at the base thereafter.

The "Trial" of Mosheh Gerber

Several days after our arrival at the base, we were called to a parade, where the Commissar read the death sentence of one of our friends, Mosheh Gerber, who had come together with our group. He had been accused of betraying his comrades and that during his questioning by the Gestapo he gave away names of comrades in the Underground. After the parade, a Russian Partisan took him behind the bathhouse and shot him. The executor came back with the murderer's man's boots in his hands. This event left a very bad impression on most of the Jewish Partisans, who had been his friend in Kovno. I could not imagine that after the horrors Mosheh went through, he would be shot by his own comrades. Only after some time did I become aware of the fact that human life among the Partisans, and especially a Jewish one, did not have much value. Many Partisans were shot by their own comrades after accusations of some minor lapses and after so called "trials." Mosheh Gerber was caught by the Lithuanian Police while taking part in the unfortunate expedition to Augustova, and found with a pistol in his pocket. He was brought to the Gestapo and after being questioned and beaten, was sent to the Ninth Fort, where he joined the group whose job it was to burn the murdered (See above). Some comrades accused him of naming the man who gave him the pistol as well as providing additional names of members of the Underground, to the Gestapo, although there was no proof that he had done so. After a brave escape from the fort, he arrived in the Ghetto and there was sentenced to death by the heads of the Underground. They did not want to execute him there, because his family lived in the ghetto, so they decided to send him to the woods. Nekhemia Endlin, who was the commander of the group, was ordered to kill him on the way, but did not agree. So it was decided to bring him to the base, where he would be judged. After arriving at the base, the Commander of the Partisan Brigade *(Jurgis)* was informed about this case, whereupon he sent an investigator to our regiment. The investigator sat for three days, with the accused and the witnesses who were in the base, and then he issued his verdict, saying that there was no real proof of Mosheh's betrayal, but if the Underground in the Ghetto had issued a death sentence, it had to be carried out.

Forty years later, most of the ex-partisans being in Israel, one of them, Zunia Shtrom, initiated the publication of a document, which everybody signed, exonerating Mosheh Gerber. A copy of it was sent to Mosheh's brother who lives in the USA.

Among about 350 people of the Underground who went out of the Ghetto, 88 were killed on different occasions.

Life in the Woods

On one of the first evenings in the base we were sitting and singing around a bonfire and my friends asked me where my harmonica was and why I had not brought it with me. In the Ghetto, in the circle of my underground friends, I played this musical instrument very often, but when we left for the woods, I had left it behind in the Ghetto. Being in the Ghetto I could not assess the contribution of a harmonica to social life in the forest. During that evening, at the bonfire, a Jewish man whose identity I did not know then or even now, came to me and asked me if I can play the harmonica. After getting my positive answer, he went away and returned after a few minutes, bringing me a new double sized "Echo" harmonica made by "Hohner" in Germany. This harmonica accompanied me throughout the "Partizanka," the short period I was in the Red Army, through my stay in Kovno after the liberation, and it was with me during my wanderings through Europe and in the ship which brought me illegally to Eretz-Yisrael. Finally I gave it to my little son Ami to play with, and bought myself a new one, the same size and from the same company. This harmonica was my personal weapon, second only to the rifle, and sometimes even more important.

The first job we had to perform in the base was to build dugouts for dwellings. First we had to dig a big pit, 20 meters long, 4-5 meters wide and 1.5 meters deep. Its walls were buttressed with poles hammered into the ground and between them we laid stumps of young trees. On both sides of the dugout we installed long planes of wood, also made from the trees, for sleeping purposes. The space between these planes was dug 0.5 meter deeper, to enable walking through without having to bend down. The roof of the dugout was covered with stumps of young trees and on them a layer of earth, hyssop and branches, as camouflage. Sometimes at night in the darkness, after sitting around the bonfire, it was very difficult to find the entrance to the dugout. On both sides of the dugout there were doors which were closed in winter. There was also an improvised oven. In summer the doors were open and swarms of mosquitoes disturbed one's sleep.

In February, when we arrived in the woods, it was still winter and sometimes snow covered the woods. Inside the dugout it was warm and those not on duties could stay in it, and as a result friendships developed among the people. According to regulations we had to sleep fully dressed and one was allowed to take off boots or shoes only. The rifle had to be at your side at all times. If anybody lost his rifle he was liable to be sentenced to death and I heard of many such incidents, but not in our regiment.

Crowding in the dugout as well as unhygienic conditions contributed to the spreading of lice. The bathhouse and sauna, which were built at the end of the base brought some relief. It was a small dugout and in it there was an oven, which heated layers of stones and by pouring water on it, we were able to get very hot steam. In this way we washed, both body and garments, and disposed of the lice. Wood for burning was plentiful and water, too. The river Merkys, a tributary of the Nieman, flowed near the base, and groundwater level was close to the surface.

A Jewish girl, who for some medical reasons was unable to participate in military activities, had the task of laundering our clothes. Together with the garments, everyone had to give her a piece of soap, which we had to obtain during procurement operations when we were with the peasants. There was also another way to change underwear. Being in a peasant's house during a requisitioning action for food, you left the peasant your dirty underwear and received clean ones from him.

We took food for the base from the peasants in the villages. Every regiment had its special region, up to 30 km. from the base, where it was allowed to expropriate the required food. These actions were executed by large groups, up to 15-25 people, and with the best weapons available. We would leave the base at sunset and walk many kilometers until we reached the designated village. At the edge of the village, patrols armed with machine guns were positioned to guard the operation, while others deployed in the village, woke the peasants and ordered some of them to harness their carts, on which we loaded the expropriated food. Mostly it was flour, pigs, grits and sometimes also cows. We told them that when the Red Army returns, they would be compensated for all the products we had taken from them. Their carts and horses would be given back to them the next day somewhere at the edge of the forest. The policy was not to impoverish the peasants completely, and if some of them had only one pig or one cow, we did not take it. It was forbidden to take superfluous things for private use. After returning tired from such an operation, the Commissar would search those who had participated. This was very humiliating and depressing and reminded one of the searches at the gate of the Ghetto.

The Commissar himself was an escaped war prisoner, a Russian with fair blond hair. His name was Davidov and often he was verbally abusive to the Jews. The Commander of the Base was Kostia Radionov Simonov, a Russian from Lithuania who, at the beginning of the war had escaped to Russia and was later parachuted into the woods. The Commander of the Brigade was, as mentioned above, G.Ziman (Jurgis). He was a Communist in the Underground during Lithuanian rule and was parachuted into the woods with the task of establishing a Lithuanian Partisan Movement. His main ambition was to prove to Moscow, that he was fulfilling his task, whereas the idea of saving more Jewish youths from extermination was not his first priority. So it was important to him that in his brigade there should be more Lithuanians and Russians than Jews.

The Jews who came to the base from the Ghetto were asked to bring rifles (not pistols), medical and other equipment. The age of newcomers was limited and so was the number of girls. One group was asked why they did not bring gold from the Ghetto for the purpose of buying weapons. On the other hand, escaped war prisoners were accepted mostly without any conditions.

The seventh group, mentioned above, consisted of 28 well-armed and equipped people, among them nine young women .Nekhemia Endlin, who at this time also the Commander of the group, left the women in one of the Vilna Jewish regiments and came to the base with the men. He reported to the Base Commander that he had left nine armed young women elsewhere, because he was ordered not to bring more women to the base. The Commander ordered one of the Partisans to go and bring all the women to the base, if only for their rifles.

All this caused bad feelings among the Jewish fighters, whose expectations were to bring more Jewish youths from the Ghetto did not come true. Also the anti-Semitism of most of the comrades in arms and in particular of the Commissar caused hard feelings.

It was for these reasons that I decided not to go back to the Lithuanian Base, when later on I was thrown into a Jewish Partisan regiment, as will be told further on.

With the "Fighting Unit"

One day a "Fighting Unit" which contained 30-40 men, half of them Jewish, was established, men from the three regiments at the base: "Death to the Invaders," "Vladas Baronas" and "Forward." I too was attached to this unit. Its Commander was Misha Trushin, a Russian Lieutenant, an escaped war prisoner. When he was in a good mood, after a few drinks of samogon *(see next page)*, he very much liked to dance to the music I played on my harmonica. I am almost sure that I was attached to this particular unit because of my musical instrument.

During the two and a half months I spent in this regiment, I participated in a few procurement operations for food and arms and also in a fighting action, in which we burned down a sawmill with all its equipment. I took part in several other actions, but these I have already forgotten.

Once, when we were on our way back from requisitioning, I received an order to accompany a Partisan, a native of a nearby village, to his home. I went along with him and in a certain house we secured a little bottle containing some fluid. He gave me the bottle and I put it in my pocket. I did not notice that the bottle leaked and while walking to the base the fluid moistened the left leg of my trousers. When I arrived at the base the left part of my trousers disintegrated and only then I realized that the bottle contained salicylic acid which was needed for the battery of the radio in headquarters. I found myself in an unpleasant situation, as there was no stock of clothes in the base, but somebody gave me a pair of trousers made of thick wool, which was a perfect habitat for lice to reproduce.

Those Partisans not on duty would gather around a bonfire in the evenings and sing. First we sang Russian songs, then Yiddish and later Hebrew Songs. There were two Hebrew dance songs which everybody in the base learned to sing. I accompanied most of the songs by playing my harmonica. During my stay in this regiment there were two Soviet holidays, the holiday of the Red Army on February 23rd and International Women's Day on March 3rd. Before these two holidays I learned to play several new songs, among them "The Sportsmen's March." I played this march hundreds of times and often the Fighting Unit marched, accompanied by this tune, when going into action. I learned to play the melodies of most of the Russian Folk Dances quite quickly, and played them at every opportunity. Sometimes when staying in a peasant's house to rest on our way back to the base, I would play and the Partisans would dance. When there were girls in the peasant's house, the joy became more intense.

Before coming to the forest, I knew nothing about alcohol. My familiarity with it was probably limited to the wine at "Kiddush." It was in the woods that I was introduced to "Samogon" for the first time. This was an alcoholic beverage similar to Vodka but with a bad smell, which the peasants made by themselves from sugar or potatoes or grains, in spite of the ban. The Russians were very eager to get Samogon, but many partisans lost their lives because of it, among them the commander of the "Fighting Unit," Misha Trushin. Once, in a peasant's house not far from the base, we were offered Samogon. I did not want to drink, but was forced to drink half a glass due to social pressure. After a short time I vomited and ever since then have not touched it again. But when you find yourself in a society in which drinking alcoholic beverages is the norm, it is very difficult not to join in, so that slowly I got used to liking Vodka and for many years since have drunk it at meetings with friends and other celebrations.

On one occasion a group of Partisans from our regiment met a convoy of carts on their way back to the base. The carts were carrying sugar for Easter to some village in the region. The Partisans turned the convoy into the woods, unloaded the sugar and released the carts. One of them reported the loot, and everyone in the base at that time went with sacks, rucksacks, pots etc. to bring the sugar to the base, as there was no road to the base, only paths for pedestrians or for riders and sugar was a rare product in those times. In the Ghetto and of course in the forest, we used saccharine to sweeten whatever we needed and now we got a tremendous quantity of sugar. All the way to the base I licked the sugar and so did everybody else. A short time after this episode, I left this base, as will be told afterwards, and I heard later that part of the sugar was given to peasants in the vicinity in exchange for Samogon.

The Goal

One day in April 1944 I was called to base headquarters and was informed that on the next day I was to join a group of 25 Partisans, chosen from all the regiments of the Brigade, for a special mission. At the time the state of the Partisan's arms in this Brigade was not satisfactory, and arms parachuted from Moscow had not arrived yet. The arms we had were mostly taken by force from the peasants. The peasants were able to get hold of them during the retreat of the Red Army at the beginning of the war. The arms also included those which we brought with us from the Ghetto, primarily purchased with money.

Partisans from our Brigade, who earlier had been sent eastwards on a mission, told the Commander after returning, that in the headquarters of the Belorussian Brigade they were told that at the airfield of that Brigade there were parachuted arms, munitions, also newspapers and proclamations written in Lithuanian. Actually all this equipment was meant for the Lithuanian Brigade, but was dropped there by mistake. Therefore it was decided by our headquarters to send a group of Partisans into the woods of Naliboki, where the headquarters of the Belorussian Brigade was situated, in order to collect the arms, which were designated for us. I learned later on, several weeks after we went on that mission that Soviet airplanes started to drop big quantities of arms, munitions, medical equipment etc. for our brigade, so that our mission was actually unnecessary. But let me continue my story.

As mentioned above, this group consisted of 25 men, among them 16 Jews from our and the Vilna regiments, eight Russians and Ukrainians and a Russian Commander.

Since our mission was to bring back good arms from Naliboki, it did not seem logical to carry good arms there and back, so we only got pistols and cut off rifles for our defense. Peasants would shorten the handle and the barrel of the rifle, so that they could hide it in their belt underneath their coat. It is impossible to make a direct hit with this type of rifle, but when fired it made a lot of noise.

The distance to Naliboki was about 150 km., mostly through hostile areas. In view of the type of group we were and the arms at our disposal, it was considered very dangerous to traverse these areas. Therefore we joined a group of 30 Partisans from a regiment named Morozov, whose base was in the woods of Naliboki and who were on their way back from a mission in Lithuania. They looked like soldiers of the regular army. They all wore uniforms and were armed with submachine guns, machine guns and also had a small caliber mortar. The Commander of the joint group was, of course, a man of the Morozov regiment. According to Partisan methods, we walked at night and rested during the day. At sunrise we would capture some village and sleep and eat there. On such a day none of the villagers were allowed to leave and anyone coming into the village was forced to stay there until after we left.

The Ultimatum of the "White Poles"

One day we rested in a village with a church and because it was Sunday, well dressed peasants from the vicinity came to pray. This was a good opportunity for some Partisans to exchange their worn out boots for better ones by taking them from the peasants. Usually there were no problems and the exchange went smoothly. On the afternoon of this day, however, our patrols brought an elderly peasant to the Commander, who delivered a letter to him. After reading the letter, the commander ordered all the Partisans to wake for a parade. There he read the letter, in Polish, the contents of which were approximately: "You are surrounded. Lay down your arms, surrender the Jews to us and then we will let you go." The letter was signed by the A.K. (Armiya Krayova). These were the so called "White Poles," who had declared total war against the Partisans and particularly against the Jews. If a non-Jewish Partisan fell into their hands, they would usually confiscate his rifle and let him go, but if it was a Jew he was shot without hesitation.

The countryside was still covered with snow and from afar we saw their concentration of sledges. The commander ordered us to move with the guidance of the peasant who brought the letter. He was told that he must take us away from there, otherwise he would be shot. Our mortar shot a few shells into the sledge concentration then we moved fast, although it was still daylight. On our way there was a small meandering stream. Most of the Partisans jumped across in one big leap, as did I, but others fell into the water several times and got wet. One of my friends (Jankl Kave) wore a short cotton filled coat and after crossing the stream several times it became so heavy that he was forced to abandon it. While running, the Poles shot at us, but no one was hurt. After we were far away from that village, we were counted and it turned out that nobody was missing. After several days we reached the woods of Naliboki without any more incidents. At the edge of the woods we saw burned and destroyed villages. This was the outcome of the great Partisan hunt in the summer of 1943, which the Germans carried out with the help of the local police and thousands of collaborators in the occupied states, Lithuanians, Latvians, Ukrainians and others. Not many Partisans were killed during this hunt, because they did not want to fight open battles against thousands of soldiers with armed cannons and who also had reconnaissance airplanes at their disposal. Thanks to the vastness of the woods and their impassable swamps, most of the Partisans managed to evade the persecutors. The major victims of that hunt were the villages on the edges of the woods. They were destroyed completely and their inhabitants were murdered or transported to Germany as forced laborers. The villages inside the woods were mostly undamaged and when we arrived there in the spring of 1944 they were under Partisan rule. The Germans and their collaborators did not dare enter them again.

We arrived in the small town of Baksht, deep in the forest, more or less unharmed. It was a Polish-Jewish town with one long street, a market square and a small stream with a wooden bridge. There were no more Jews in the town. The experience of walking on the sidewalk with the short rifle on my shoulder was intense. Only two months ago I had left the Ghetto after almost three years of suppression and abuse, and here I suddenly was a free man, walking in daylight without fear, without the yellow patches and armed with a rifle, if a funny one, but still a rifle. Apparently my stay in the Lithuanian base had not allowed me to feel free.

After arriving in Baksht, we took leave of Morozov's men and our Commander, and together with another Partisan, went to the headquarters of the Bielorussian Brigade, and we had to wait for him. Where could we wait? We were sent to one of the villages in the region, where two persons were allotted to each peasant. There we ate and slept. In every village there was a Commandant from the Partisans who was responsible for everything. The Partisans even helped the peasants with their agricultural work. After a week we were sent to another village and so on.

With the Jewish Regiments of Belsky and Zorin

In one of these villages one evening, we saw a few carts outside a house and a lot of noise emanating from it. As we drew nearer we saw a group of Partisans eating and drinking. We would not enter the house without being invited inside, but after hearing some of them speaking Yiddish, we introduced ourselves and the joy was great. We spent a pleasant time together, ate and drank, sang songs in Yiddish and Hebrew and even danced the "Hora." By way of questions and answers we found out that these people belonged to the Jewish regiment of the Brothers Belsky and that they were on their way to their base after fulfilling some task. For the first time we heard that there existed, in the woods of Naliboki, a so-called "Family Regiment" and in it 1,200 Jewish men, women and children. They told us also that near their base there is another "Family Regiment," with 700 Jews from Minsk whose Commander was named Zorin. I have to point out that in those days every Jew thought that he and the people around him were the only ones who had survived, and this meeting was therefore a very exciting experience. Several friends and I decided on the spot to join them and not to return to our regiment. I discussed this with the commander of the Belsky men and he, in a good mood after the vodka he had drunk, agreed to take us with him. He said, "go to sleep now and come to me in the morning." When I and my partner at that time A. Feitelson, returned to our place, an argument ensued. First, whether we, the Jews, should be the first ones to disrupt our group, or whether we should we wait until the "goyim" would do so, secondly, what would our commanders in Lithuania say etc, etc. This argument lasted half way through the night. Nevertheless, I stuck to my view that I would settle the account with my commander after the war, but now I wanted to be among Jews. In the morning we came to the Belsky men, but their commander, having sobered up during the night, decided that he had no authority to bring alien Partisans to his base. He suggested we come to their base for a visit and explained how to get there.

Meanwhile our commander returned from headquarters and told us that there were no arms there for us. It was true that arms had been dropped there for the Lithuanian Partisans by mistake, but they did not keep an arsenal of arms. These arms were divided up among the Partisans, whose job it was to guard the airfield at that time. If we wanted, we could go there and guard the airfield, and when more arms would eventually be dropped, we would get our share of them.

Our commander decided that there was no reason to stay here and that we would have to return to Lithuania. It was also clear that with the arms we had, we could not risk going on our own, so we would have to wait for a bigger group of well armed Partisans which would head in our direction. Meanwhile we were to remain in the villages and eat bread for nothing.

The First of May Celebration

It was the end of April and May 1st. A great holiday in the Soviet Union was approaching. We asked our commander to allow us to celebrate this holiday with the Jewish regiments. He gave us his permission and also a document to avoid problems when meeting other Partisans. The 16 Jews of the group started out and after walking for two days we arrived at the Belsky regiment (Officially the *regiment in the name of "Kalinin").* The night during our march we spent with a few Jewish families who lived in a dugout and did not belong to any organized group. These Jews had a hard life, because they had been robbed and also murdered by the Partisans. Most of those who did not join the Partisans did not survive.

Arriving at the Belsky Regiment, we assembled at first in its headquarters, where we were met by Commander Tuviyah Belsky, Chief of Staff Malbin, and the Commander of the Fighting Group Asael Belsky, all brave men wearing nice uniforms. They asked us who we were and where we came from and were surprised that only two months ago we had left the Kovno Ghetto and that there were still Jews there. They had heard that there had been no Jews in the towns and villages for quite some time. They warmly welcomed us and invited us to participate in the First of May celebrations. We asked if we could stay on with them, to which they answered that they had no objection, but would have to get approval from Brigade headquarters.

Inside the camp of this regiment there were several streets with dugouts and huts. During winter the people lived in these dugouts, whereas in summer they lived in the huts, with roofs made from the bark of trees. In the middle of the camp there stood a big shed, which housed the workshops. These consisted of a blacksmith and a locksmith's shop, which also repaired arms and refilled the cartridges of the Russian pistol, the "Nagan," because for some reason there were not enough bullets for it. There were also shops for carpenters, tailors, shoemakers and cobblers. In addition there were several bathhouses, a hospital, a disinfecting house, workshops for making soap, for sausages, for leather, a bakery, a cemetery, a jail and a synagogue. There was also a school for children, with two women teachers and a few Rabbis and Yeshiva students who sat and studied "Torah," of which Tuviyah was very proud.

In addition to these there was the headquarters building, several bunkers, stables for the horses and a cowshed.

Several Jewish doctors and many nurses worked in the hospital. The workshops served the entire Bielorussian Brigade. The commanders of the different regiments would come here for their uniforms and boots, to repair saddles and harnesses for the horses, to repair their arms and to refill the "Nagan" cartridges. For example, they would bring cattle and in exchange get sausage. They paid, of course, for the services they received, either with some produce or with explosives, arms and munitions. The high officers, whose help Belsky wanted, sometimes got presents from him.

The First of May celebration took place in the above-mentioned big shed. A stage was constructed and a short show in Yiddish was performed. There were speeches in Russian and Yiddish and a choir sang. But the climax was a group of little boys and girls, who danced the popular Jewish Dance "Sherele" to the well known melody sung by the choir. Even today it is difficult to explain the emotion I, and I believe also my friends felt seeing a group of Jewish children singing and dancing in those horrible times. For years after this event I have had tears in my eyes when telling about it.

Tuviyah and Lilka Belsky

Asa'el and Khayah Belsky

A dwelling dugout of the Partisans in Rudniky woods
Courtesy of Nancy Lefkowitz (May 2001)

The Belsky Family

Father and Mother Belsky had seven sons and several daughters. They lived in the town of Novogrudek in the northeastern part of Poland. The family was the owner of a mill, where they ground flour and grits for Polish and Bielorussian peasants. The sons Tuviyah, Zusia, Asael and their young brother Aharon had never been in a Ghetto and had never worn the yellow patches. From the beginning of the German occupation they hid in the woods of this area. At first, it was only a hiding place, but after they saw the mass murders of the Jews in the surrounding towns, they started to organize, to evacuate members of the family and other relatives from the ghettoes and to gather together Jews who had escaped into the woods. The father, the mother and two other sons of the family, when ill, were caught by the Germans and murdered.

The brothers acquired arms and defended themselves against the many enemies surrounding them. They had to overcome many difficulties and unfortunately paid with the loss of many lives until they were recognized by the Bielorussian headquarters as a Partisan regiment. Only Tuviyah's standing and wisdom enabled this regiment to survive. In the spring of 1943, during the German's great hunt of the Partisans, as told above, most of the Belsky people were rescued, thanks to a Jewish man, a native of this region, who knew the woods very well. He convoyed most of the people through the swamps to an island in the forest, which the Germans and their helpers did not frequent. At the end of the hunt, with only a few losses among the Partisans, the Jews who had dispersed in the forests, gathered together, and so the Belsky regiment, which numbered about 1,200 persons, was established. According to Partisan terminology, this was a "Family Regiment," and another "Fighting Regiment" had to protect it and look after its needs. This "Fighting Regiment" so called in the name of Ordzenikidze, the name of a famous communist leader. Its commander was Zusia Belsky, but actually the Tuviyah regiment was independent, thanks to its "industry," and he even organized a "Fighting Group" with Asael as its commander. When we arrived there in the spring of 1944, the situation in the regiment was already pretty good. There were arms, food, and it seemed that the end of the war was close. The Germans and their collaborators did not dare enter these woods, where there was absolute Soviet rule. The most dangerous enemy was the "White Poles," who circulated throughout the woods with relative freedom.

The brothers Zusia, Tuviyah and Aharon Belsky arrived in Eretz-Yisrael immediately after the war. Several years later the entire family immigrated to America. During their stay in the country their book "Yehudei Ya'ar" (Jews of Woods) was published by "Sifriath

Poalim," in Tel Aviv in 1946. Asael Belsky had enlisted in the Red Army and was killed in battle. His widow Khaya and daughter Asaelah arrived in Eretz-Yisrael and still live here. Tuviyah died in America and was buried in Jerusalem.

Shalom Zorin

The day after the celebrations in the Belsky regiment, we were invited to visit the regiment of the Minsk Jews, whose commander was Shalom Zorin. This regiment, as mentioned before, consisted of about 700 people, mostly from Minsk. Zorin, who had already been a Partisan in the civil war in Russia, was a simple man with a warm Jewish heart. He picked up every Jew he met in the woods and after significant efforts in the headquarters of the Bielorussian Brigade, was recognized as the commander of this "Family Regiment," called "Unit 106." He obtained 15 rifles and several grenades and was advised to move from the vicinity of Minsk into the Naliboky woods, where it was safer and easier for unarmed civilians to survive.

Many Jewish youngsters, who had escaped from the Minsk Ghetto, joined different Partisan regiments. It is noteworthy to mention a group of children aged 11-15, who went many times from the woods to the Ghetto in Minsk. They served as guides to the Zorin regiment for the hundreds of Jewish people who managed to escape from the Ghetto.

After arriving in their camp, we were impressed by the Jewish youth who grew up under Soviet rule. It was a holiday and it was very jolly. They sang and danced well. There were many very nice girls among them and a few of them excelled in dancing the Russian folkdances. My harmonica helped to entertain the dancers, as there was no other musical instrument. Their camp was similar to that of the Belsky regiment and there were also some workshops which helped to maintain this big community. The main task of Zorin and his staff was to ensure the lives of the 700 Jewish people in his regiment and to take them out safely from the woods. The responsibility of obtaining provisions was given to a group of about 20 armed men, who had to travel distances to collect food from peasants.

After staying a few days with the Zorin regiment, we walked back to the village we had come from. The commander and another Partisan of our group went to headquarters for a second time to ask for an armed group we could join on its way to Lithuania. Several days later the Partisan returned without the commander. He said that on their way there the Germans bombed the area, a splinter hit the commander's head and he died. We had no choice but to believe this story, in spite of our suspicion that this Partisan killed the commander for some reason. It should be mentioned here that human life in the woods was very cheap.

Our group did not belong to anyone in this area and there was no real authority where we could bring our concerns and ask for an investigation. The death of our commander resulted in a new situation in our group. Several Partisans among the Russians and the Ukrainians of our group also wanted to stay there and not return to their regiments. They had found a few "Family Regiments" in the vicinity that included many young women and so they wanted to stay there. Among the 16 Jews, six expressed their wish to stay with the Belsky regiment, but we did not want to be the first to announce this and disrupt our group. One day a young Ukrainian, who had taken over command, gathered the group, made them stand in line and said that whoever wants to stay should take one step forward. I do not remember how many Russians stepped forward, but six of the Jews did, as mentioned before. So we said good bye to our friends and went to join the Belsky regiment, where we handed over our poor arms and got proper rifles instead. We were dispersed throughout several dugouts and began to acclimate. I was put into a dugout where several tens of men and women lived. They were sleeping on shelves along the walls. After a few weeks there we were called to the commander, who told us that according to an order from headquarters we were to be transferred to the Zorin regiment, because there were not enough young fighters. We did not regret this very much, in spite of the fact that we had joined the Belsky regiment, who were "Litvaks," whereas in the Zorin regiment there were Soviet Jews who were educated differently than us.

The Zorin regiment was situated, as mentioned above, on the other side of a path which divided it from the Belsky regiment. Also there we were dispersed among several dugouts, and became regular Partisans of that regiment. Meeting these youth was very interesting, as prior to meeting us they had never heard of the Hebrew language, of Eretz-Yisrael, or of Zionism. They were also disappointed by the education they had received in Soviet schools, because their schoolmates suddenly became Jew killers. I should point out that the mood in that regiment was joyous. I played my harmonica, to which the Minsk youths danced on every occasion, and also learned the two Hebrew dance melodies from me, as I mentioned before.

After several weeks the regiment got an order to move to another place, nearer to the swamps. The "Family Regiment" was positioned in one place and the quasi-fighting group, numbering about 20 men, in another place, about one kilometer away from the families. We built huts there, and in each of them housed three men and one girl, whose job it was to cook our food and be the hostess.

When the fighting group went to visit the families or on some mission, I was in the first row playing marches with my harmonica and the group marched to its rhythm. During the month and a half I was in this regiment, I took part in food procurement operations several times. Each Partisan regiment had its allotted region where it was allowed to take food from the peasants. This arrangement was made to prevent the peasants from starving, and since the nearby villages were already under Partisan rule, it was forbidden to take anything from them. On the contrary, they received help from the Partisans. The villages on the edge of the woods had been destroyed by the Germans, their population murdered or sent to Germany as forced labor, so only villages which were several tens of km. from the base remained where we could take provisions. To these villages we had to travel during the night and return before dawn.

The first time I took part in such an operation, we sat in carts drawn by horses and the convoy traveled on a road towards its task. I asked one of the veterans whether there was the usual patrol in front of the convoy, to which he replied that their patrol is God himself.

One afternoon, in the beginning of July 1944, I was in the "Family Regiment" on the occasion of some celebration. I was playing my harmonica and the young people were dancing. Suddenly a partisan a guard, appeared. He told us that there were Germans in the vicinity. Commander Zorin went ahead with a group of fighters in the direction the guard had pointed, and I also went along with this group, as in addition to my haromonica I also had a rifle. Not far from the "Family Regiment" there was a big swamp that looked like a meadow. The entire area of the swamp was green because of the vegetation covering the water. In the swamp itself there were a few "islands" and on them we saw several German soldiers. Zorin stood up straight, shouting to them to surrender, but in reply they opened fire. Zorin's legs were wounded and a few Partisans were killed. The two German soldiers who were there were caught, brought to the base and shot after a short investigation.

The days after that incident were very unpleasant. Shots from different directions were heard and we had no idea who was doing the shooting. The frontline was approaching fast, German soldiers were escaping through the woods in groups or as individuals, and sometimes there were encounters and even victims. The Germans were very afraid of the Partisans, because they knew that they did not take any prisoners.

When he was old, in the 1970's, Zorin came to Israel. I was present at the welcoming party, arranged in his honor in Kibbutz Lokhamei Hagetaoth *(Ghetto Fighters Kibbutz)*. A short time after that he passed away.

My comrades in arms from the partisans regiment at Rudniky woods
First line below from left: Shimon Blokh *, Moshe Sherman *
Second line from left: M.Lipkovitz, Alte Borokhovitz-Teper *, David Teper,
Rivkah Blokh *, Sh.Broier
Third line: Yehudah Eidelman *, Zunia Shtrom *,A.Gafanovitz
Fourth line: Yakov Ratner, A. Shtrom, Eliezer Zilber, L.Zaitsev *, Dov Shtern,
Y.Yukhnikov

Most of them came to Israel during the 1970s and a number of them passed away in Israel (*)

Ex-Partisans: Khayim Galeen, Grisha Shefer and Josef Rosin
Alba-Julia 1945   Nofit 1993

The Departure from the Woods

One day we received an order to leave the base and move in the direction of Minsk. All the horses we had were harnessed to the carts and on them we laid Zorin and the other wounded as well as our food supplies, including a few cows which were tied to the carts. Thus the convoy left the woods, while all the people went on foot. After half a day we met the first soldiers of the Red Army. There were embraces and kisses and also a few speeches. We continued until we arrived in the town of Kuidonovo on the way to Minsk, where we met a convoy of military trucks which was on its way from the frontline to Minsk.

We got permission to climb onto these trucks, leaving all we possessed in that town except for our arms, and arrived in Minsk. The citizens of Minsk among us went to find their former apartments and we, the "Lithuanians," joined a Minsk citizen who found his flat completely empty. Apparently it had been occupied by Germans who managed to escape together with the army. There we found shelter and a floor to sleep on. The big problem we had to face was the lack of food.

In Minsk

Minsk had been liberated a short time before we arrived, and there was much chaos in the city. At night the Germans still bombed the city and I was witness to the bombing of the railway station, when a train loaded with ammunition exploded like a spectacular fireworks show. Law and order in the city was not organized as yet and it was impossible to buy food. The situation was made even worse since we did not have even one ruble. Thousands of Partisans from the Bielorussian woods started to arrive in the city, but they did not make the mistake the commanders of the Zorin regiment had made. They arrived in the city with all their equipment and the provisions they had and until they were disbanded they lived together as they lived in the woods. The people of our regiment, including its commanders, were mostly citizens of Minsk and were impatient to return "home" so they did not evaluate the situation in the city correctly and therefore had left all the provisions we had in Kuidonovo. Consequently, we starved. We went about the streets with our rifles in our hands, knocked on doors and asked for something to eat, like beggars. Luckily we still had our rifles and the population, still shocked by the liberation from the Nazis, wanted to help the hungry Partisans. Without the rifles and the way I looked, I would have died of hunger. The German boots I got in the Ghetto before my departure to the woods had served me very well all this time. But a short time before leaving the woods the sole of the left boot disintegrated, leaving only the upper part. If this had happened earlier, my boot would have been repaired at the shoemaker shop in the regiment, but it happened when the big attack of the Red Army started and chaos began in the woods, as mentioned above, and it was impossible to get the necessary help. In a peasant's house I found a small mat (Lapche in Yiddish) which the poor peasants wore instead of shoes, and tied it to my left foot with some cord. Thus I walked with one whole boot and one with a mat instead of a sole.

Meanwhile several hard weeks passed and we were told that a committee from Moscow had arrived, whose task it was to disband the Partisan regiments and that our turn would come soon. We were also told that on a certain day there would be a parade of all the Partisans, where the salute would be taken by the member of the Politbureau (The Head Office of the Communist Party in USSR) who was in charge of the Partisan Movement (Ponomarenko ?). The parade took place in a big square in the city with the participation of tens of thousands of Partisans. The different clothes, mostly worn out, arms of different origins and even light guns and mortar which some regiments had, made it look more like a carnival then a military parade. I also participated in it, wearing my strange looking boots.

Заслуженному воину-партизану
Второй Мировой войны

לוחם - פרטיזן
במלחמת העולם השנייה

Фамилия : Розин

שם משפחה: רוזין

Имя : Иосиф

שם פרטי: יוסף

Отчество :

Дата выдачи: 18.6.95

תאריך הוצאה: 18.6.1995

Верховный Совет Белоруссии

הסוביט העליון של הרפובליקה הביילורוסית

Союз Партизанов и Повстанцев
гетто в Израиле

ארגון הפרטיזנים ולוחמי הגיטאות בישראל

Председатель:　　Секретарь:
Моше Калхейм　　Яков Гриншейн
M. Kale　　Я. Гриншейн

מזכיר　　יו"ר הארגון
יעקב גרינשטיין　　משה קלכהיים

The medal from the Belarus Government

МЕДАЛЬ ЖУКОВА

Б № 0971322

РОЗИН

ИОСЕФ

НАГРАЖДЕН(А)

МЕДАЛЬЮ ЖУКОВА

Президент
Российской Федерации

Указ от „........"...................... 19 ..... года

Marshal Zhukov Medal granted by the Russian Federation

The parade was filmed and my friend A.Feitelson saw the film some years later in Kovno.

In 1995, together with more ex-partisans, I received a medal and a certificate from the Belarus government for my participation as a Partisan fighter in WWII.

A few years later I received the Marshal Zhukov medal with a certificate from the government of the Russian Federation. Marshal Zhukov was the High Commander of the forces which liberated Belarus, Lithuania etc. and reached Berlin where he accepted the surrender of the German Army.

The Enlistment into the Red Army

In due course it was our turn and we stood before the committee. It became clear that after handing over the rifle and getting a certificate (without a photo) stating that you had participated as a Partisan in some regiment in The Great Homeland War, you were enlisted into the Army or mobilized for work for different jobs of the building branch. We, the "Lithuanian" group, approached the officers of the committee, told them who we were and that we wanted to return to Lithuania. We told them that we had been cut off from our Lithuanian regiment and that we did not know what had happened to our relatives in the Kovno Ghetto and therefore asked to go back to Lithuania. Unfortunately, all our explanations did not help and we found ourselves enlisted into the Red Army. We were taken to a military camp outside the city and were housed there in four story buildings. We also had to pass some drill exercises. We did not get uniforms and were left with our own clothes, including the lice. There was not enough food and I was hungry. One evening, after a week or so, we were taken to a long cargo train, one platoon per wagon, which started to move. A commander was appointed in every wagon and battle rations were divided among us. It was summer and the sky was clear, so according to the stars I calculated that we were going westwards, i.e. in the direction of Lithuania and this gave me some consolation. When military trains that carried equipment and provisions to the front overtook us, our train was shunted to a side track, so that the other trains could pass without any delay. Thus our journey from Minsk to Vilna continued for several days, instead of several hours under normal conditions. Sometimes, when our train stopped for a few hours, the soldiers jumped down and cooked something from the battle rations they had. Once, I remember, a soldier wanted to add potatoes, which he had seen in a nearby field, to his soup. He stepped on a mine, which exploded and it killed him.

Sadly, he had forgotten that the Germans had planted mines along hundreds of kilometers of the railway tracks to protect them against the Partisans.

We passed Vilna and continued to move westwards. At the station of Koshedar (Kaisiadorys), which is situated half way between Kovno and Vilna, the train stopped and we disembarked. Three years before, as I have told above, at the beginning of the war, my friend Moshe Vald and I, climbed onto a train in this very station, which took us to the outskirts of Vilna on our aborted attempt to escape to Russia.

Now a group of officers from different units of the Red Army waited for us and then they collected the number of soldiers allocated to him. I found myself in a group called the "Tancodessants." They were infantry, attached to the armored corps, of which one section sat on each tank, mostly T-34's, armed with submachine guns. They advanced together with the tanks and in battle they had to jump off the tank and advance behind or beside it. They then had to hold the positions that the tank captured. The officer who adopted us made a fiery speech about the great luck and honor we had received by belonging to the Katelnikovsky Corps *(Katelnikovo-a village in the vicinity of Stalingrad, where these corps held certain positions which stopped the Germans from breaking through the encirclement)* and to the 19th Gvardeisky Brigade. Only units that had distinguished themselves in battle were accepted into this Gvardiya, and its soldiers received a particular emblem on their uniforms.

We had to stand in line and a sergeant major passed from one to another and decided what part of the uniform everyone would get. I got boots with rubber soles and tarpaulin bootlegs, trousers, underwear and a service cap. I do not remember if I was handed a shirt too, but before that we were ordered to wash in a pond which was near the railway. So I got rid of my rough trousers with the lice as well as the funny boot and finally became a real soldier. Nearby there was a tent camp, where we were housed and employed in different services. We were told that we had to wait for the arrival of tanks. Meanwhile there was not much to do and for the first time I read a small book in Russian that I found somewhere, with Chekhov stories.

At the Front

One day the tanks arrived, each infantry section was attached to a tank and underwent some training. The soldiers climbed onto the tank, jumped off and this was all the training given. I was then on duty in the kitchen and did not participate in this training episode. The next morning we climbed onto the tanks and moved westwards. After the great success of the spring offensive in 1944, when the Red Army captured Belorussia and half of Lithuania, the frontline became stagnant for about half a year, with Lithuania cut in half. Vilna and Kovno were liberated, but the western parts of the state were still in German hands, which were only captured by the Red Army after hard battles. Our Brigade moved towards the front in the direction of the city of Rasein (Raseiniai). The tanks moved slowly, and a convoy that included the kitchen, trucks with ammunition and the workshop, accompanied us. Our tank broke down and stopped. The workshop arrived immediately and started to repair it. Meanwhile the Brigade moved on and we were left behind. Our commander was a sergeant, a battle veteran, of Tatarian origin. He was experienced enough not to hurry to the front and the next day, after it became clear that our tank would not move so soon, we started to walk on foot in order to find our Brigade. It took about a week until we found it and by then we were on the frontline. We were attached to another tank, which was on the move. When the tank stopped, we, the submachine gun section, had to dig a big pit for the tank for its protection and foxholes for ourselves. Sometimes, after finishing the digging, the tank crew received an order to change its location, and there the digging would start all over again. We received food twice a day, at dawn and in the evening after dark, in order to enable the kitchen to come near to us and not to endanger it too much. In the morning we had dry food for the whole day and in the evening a good soup. The soup was brought in a bucket for the entire section, with everyone milling around, mostly on their knees, in order to ladel some soup with a personal spoon from this bucket. My spoon was made of wood and I kept it in my bootleg. Without the personal spoon one could not participate in the meal, so the spoon was almost as important as the rifle.

We received our baptism by fire one bright day sitting on the tanks when moving out of a grove into a stubble field we saw large heaps of straw. Before we understood what was happening, we heard explosions and six of our tanks were burning. The Germans and their guns were hidden in these straw heaps. My tank was not hit and it was able to turn back and we escaped.

We moved from one position to another and when it was quiet and all the soldiers were sitting in their foxholes, I took my harmonica and played the Soviet songs I knew, to the joy of the soldiers who could hear me.

One day the commander sent me and two other soldiers on a patrol mission. In a grove not far from our positions there were a few houses and we had to check if there were Germans in them. We advanced slowly, mostly crawling, to the houses, which we found empty. Suddenly a shell hit the corner of the house in which we were standing and exploded, the splinters wounded one of us. We returned to our positions carrying the wounded on the tarpaulin that every soldier received to protect himself against rain.

During this time I became familiar for the first time with a "Katiusha." It was then a secret weapon and the soldiers spoke of its marvels. I saw the trucks with the launchers behind us and after launching the 48 missiles with tremendous noise, they departed quickly. It really made a great impression on all of us.

After several weeks we were ordered to move north. Near the city of Shavl (Siauliai) hard battles were being fought and our brigade was sent to help. We climbed onto the tanks and started to move. After some time our tank broke down and stopped. The brigade moved along, whereas we and the team on the tank remained behind.

The mechanics and their tools arrived and said that it would take a few days to repair the tank. The kitchen and provisions advanced with the Brigade and we were left without food. Our commander knew that I knew Lithuanian and sent me with another soldier to get some food from farmers in the vicinity, but as I reported before, there were almost no agricultural villages in Lithuania. A farmer would build his house and farm buildings on his land, as a result of which the distance between one farmer and his neighbor was considerable. Conventional villages could be found in the center of a region, where there would be a church and also shops. I went with the other soldier, and we brought food from a farmer for the whole group. During that night I reviewed my situation. I did not know for sure what had happened to my family. Maybe someone had managed to hide and survive. I also had no idea of the fate of the Kovno Ghetto after I had left relatives, friends and also a girlfriend there. I thought about my contribution to the war against the Germans, and that if I were killed nobody would even know where I had disappeared. I had seen how easy it was to get killed, and having been a candidate for murder every hour for three years, I very much wanted to survive. The idea of leaving the army began to form in my mind. The conditions for that decison was right. I was in Lithuania, I knew the language, and I estimated that my friends from the Lithuanian Partisan regiment would by now be holding important jobs in Kovno.

The next morning our commander asked me to bring food for our section. He did not even ask another soldier to accompany me. I saw this as approval from heaven for my decision, and walked into a farm with a big courtyard, in which there was a big barn, a stable etc, surrounded by fields. I spoke to the owner, a big man with broad shoulders, and told him that I was a Lithuanian Jew, that I did not know what happened to my family and that I wanted to look for them. I offered him my arms, my uniform and my boots in exchange for civilian trousers, a shirt and shoes. He accepted my offer and I changed into my new clothes and waited in his barn until evening.

Acting on his advice I reached the main road. Meanwhile it became dark and it was dangerous to move outdoors. I saw a house by the roadside, which some passersby had entered. I went in and spent the night there. The next morning I asked someone how to continue on my way, whereupon he told me that on the previous evening, when he saw me, he thought that I was a German war prisoner who had escaped from a camp. My entire appearance, with cut hair and clothes that did not fit, really made me look suspicious. It would have been the irony of fate to be arrested as a German. I should mention that I did not have a document stating that I was a soldier, because I never received one. The only document I had was the certificate from the Belorussian Partisan headquarters, which did not have a photo.

After a few hours I arrived in Kelm (Kelme), a town which housed a famous "Yeshivah" before the war, and where my grandfather's family, Leibovitz-Braude came from many years ago.

I would like to mention now, that after I had been in Kovno for several weeks I asked my friend Ze'ev Pak, who lived in Moscow, to enquire at Army headquarters about the whereabouts of his friend Joseph Rosin, who, to the best of his knowledge, was enlisted in the army. The answer he got was that there was no such name on their lists.

Chapter 8: Back in Kovno
(August 1944-March 23, 1945)

On the market square in Kelm (Kelme) there were military trucks with drivers who looked like Jews. In fact they were Georgians or Caucasians. I asked them if maybe they were driving in the direction of Kovno and if I could go with them. They were actually going in that direction and the trucks were empty, so I sat in one of them and after several hours we entered Kovno, on the road which ran along the Ghetto fence. The view I saw gave me a tremendous shock. The whole Ghetto had been burnt down. Only the chimneys, built of bricks stood out above the ruins. As I was told later, the Germans had moved all the Jews who were still in the Ghetto and transported them to Germany, some on barges on the Nieman and by way of the sea, others on freight wagons by train. The total number of Jews in the Ghetto and in the Labor Camps had been about 10,000. The deportations started on July 8, 1944. A few thousands hid on that day in the "Malinas," specially constructed for such an occasion. After several days, when the Gestapo man in charge of the Ghetto realized that a few thousand Jews were missing, he brought units of the Gestapo and the SS into the Ghetto, among them sappers, and systematically they blew up house after house. Most of them were made of wood and they burned like torches. They also blew up four story buildings that were built of concrete. The majority of people who had hidden in the "Malinas" were burned or choked to death. People who left the "Malinas" after smoke and fire surrounded them, were shot and thrown into the flames. About 1,500 people found their death in the "Malinas." Only a few "Malinas," built beneath the four story houses, remained intact and their inhabitants survived. In the particular "Malina" I had helped to construct, all my friends who hid died.

Three weeks after the destruction of the Ghetto, on August 1, 1944, Kovno was liberated by the Red Army. I arrived in Kovno at the end of that month. I walked on Freedom Avenue, the main street of the city, and recalled, that three years before I had walked there as a student of the University with my friends, boys and girls, with the backing of a warm home which cared for all my needs. Now I returned alone, hardly dressed, without a penny and looking at passersby for a familiar face. It was not difficult to recognize Jews in the street, as their appearance and their looks easily betrayed them. I embraced and kissed every Jew I met that day, although they were unknown to me. I was told that in a house in the city a Jewish Center had been established and that there were lists of all the Jews who had returned to Kovno. I went there and found out which of my friends were in the city, at the same time adding my name to the list. Thus I met my friends, who had returned from my Partisan regiment and also those who hid in villages with Lithuanian people. Among them were Yonah and Khana Rokhman and Masha Rabinovitz with her mother. Several girls who belonged to the Underground in the Ghetto and were not allowed to join the Partisans, had managed to escape from the Ghetto and were supplied with forged documents in different villages with the help of the Lithuanian priest Paukstys. Among these were Penina Sukenik-Gofer, Mira Buz, Rachel Zagai, Rachel Rosntsvaig-Levin and others. Masha Rabinovitz and her mother the dentist invited me to live with them in the flat they had on Donelaicio Street 4a. This was a one story house, with four rooms and a kitchen. Masha and her mother, a former Kovno citizen, a woman, and myself in a separate room, all lived here. The flat was too big for three women according to the usual norms, so they were glad that I agreed to live with them, quite apart from the fact that it was good to have a man in the house. They arranged a bed and bed linen for me, and so I had a roof over my head.

A Place of Work

Now I had to worry about how to make a living. I went to Engineer Dushauskas, who was mentioned earlier, and told him about my problem. I also cared about the Landau family, knowing that the family had been deported to Germany, with the exception of the two daughters, who had been lodging with farmers in some villages. Mr. Dushauskas, despite the fact that he was arrested in 1940 by the Soviets because he had been a high official in the Lithuanian semi-fascist government, was able to get his job back as the Chief Engineer of the Post Office. The Germans also had arrested him for hiding Jews. He offered me work as a draftsman in the Post Office and a few days later I started to work there. A few weeks later I realized that I was working on a level equivalent to a mailman, and that this job was not indispensable, so that I could be called up to the army at any time. Meanwhile my friend Yonah Rochman began to work in the Road Department of the Ministry for Internal Affairs. Their chief was staff sergeant Gedalyah Levovitz Shapira, who had once told us that he was not Jewish in spite of his name and his face. At my request Yonah asked him if he needed another draftsman and after learning that he did need another worker, I left the Post Office and switched over to the Road Department. As mentioned before, this Department belonged to the Ministry of Internal Affairs, NKVD in Russian, to which the Security Police also belonged.

We, of course, had no connection with the Police, but the red pad we got with the imprinted golden letters NKVD made the needed impression, which we exploited sometimes in order to walk at night after curfew hours and also in other cases.

This job was important and there was no danger of enlistment. There were still the problems of clothes and food, with winter approaching, and I was still wearing the linen clothes I had received from the farmer.

My friends told me that some clothes had arrived, apparently from the USA, to be distributed among the ex-Partisans. I went to a certain place, where the former commander of my regiment, together with a Jewish boy by the name of David Teper, a veteran communist and once a member of the same regiment, who has been in Israel since the 1970's, indeed distributed the clothing. I only got a thin brown sweater. I was a little afraid to face the commander of the regiment, because I had remained in the Naliboki woods and did not return to his unit, but they treated me well and did not say anything.

The office I worked in received a parcel of winter clothes which included trousers, short coats and hats with ear protection, all in bright blue and filled with cotton. I asked for such a set and it was given one, which helped save me from the oncoming cold weather. The lack of food still remained a difficult problem. Food was distributed by ration cards in those days, but office workers like me got very little, and with my monthly salary I could buy only two kg of bread on the black market. The government then announced a war loan and so my salary was reduced even further. The war was still on and there was a big demand for blood donations, encouraged by notices in the city. Each donor was paid and also received additional food coupons, so I did not hesitate and became a regular donor. Every six weeks I donated, if I am not mistaken, 400 cubic cm. of blood. The money and the food I received allowed me to survive.

Yonah and I were the only two employees in the Department for Specific Construction at the Road Office. Our boss was a Lithuanian engineer, a disabled ex-serviceman, whom we hardly saw. He and the chief of the supply section used to drink day and night, and were not seen in the office. Yonah and I had nothing to do, so we sat in the office, spending our time reading. In the drawer of the table we kept "All Bialik's Poems," *(Khayim Nakhman Bialik – the national poet and writer)* a big book, which our friends gave us. We were very naive and did not realize the danger of keeping this book. Many Jews had been sent to Siberia during Stalin's time for keeping Hebrew books. How this book was preserved is a story in itself. In the Ghetto in February 1942, the Nazis had ordered the handing over of all books in all languages, including books on religion, science, fiction etc. As usual, every order from the Nazis was accompanied with a threat of the death penalty. Most people handed over their books, others burned them. Only a group from the "Bnei Zion" (ABZ) youth organization hid some Hebrew books in the ground. After Kovno was liberated from the Nazis, a few members of ABZ who had managed to survive, went to the ruins of the Ghetto and dug out the books they had hidden. Some of these books were a little worse for wear, such as the book of Bialik's poems, where the binding was damaged, but the pages were in good condition. These books passed from one person to another and so we received this and also other books, which helped us pass the time in the office.

Life in Kovno

The small group of Zionist youth, now without families, selected a few empty flats in the city and lived in them together. We met there in the evenings and sometimes arranged parties. Here I have to point out that the desire to live is stronger than anything and despite all that we had been through; we attempted to live a "normal" life. I remember a Chanukah party, which took place in one of those flats and lasted all night, with "latkes" and dancing to music that I provided playing my harmonica. At night there was a curfew, so that we would go to work directly from the parties.

On New Year's Eve of 1945 we arranged a party in the house in which I lived. Almost all my friends who were in Kovno came to the party. I cannot remember where the refreshments came from, but I do remember well where we were able to get the Vodka. One of the girl's brother's in our company was appointed director of a spirit factory, so Khayim Gal'in and I went to him and we were able to secure two bottles of Vodka. At midnight we welcomed the New Year of 1945 and our friend Grisha Shefer, who was a policeman, let off shots of joy into the air. It was a very jolly party, we sang, we danced and had a good time until dawn.

After it became clear to me that I was really quite alone, I decided to contact my Uncle Barukh in Tel Aviv. I did not remember his address, so I wrote to him at the "Herzliyah" High School in Tel Aviv. I sent two postcards immediately and on September 1, 1944 sent a long letter written in Yiddish in which I described my and our family's history, as well as the whole of Lithuanian Jewry's history during those terrible years of Nazi rule. My uncle saved that letter and gave it to me, when I finally arrived in Eretz-Yisrael. (*Tables 11, 11a, 11b, 11c and 11d are photocopies of it).* In my letter I also hinted at the fact that I had no clothes and shoes. After a month or so I received a parcel from my Uncle, but the trousers and the shoes were too small for me, so I sold them on the black market and the money I received made my situation easier. Thereafter I received two more parcels from my uncle, but no letter.

I did not go to visit Kibart. I did not wish to see the town where I had grown up and where I had a happy childhood, now in the absence of my parents, my sister and my friends. I hated that place. I was glad to hear that the house we lived in and the surrounding quarter had been destroyed during the battles between the retreating Germans and the Red Army in the summer of 1944.

Meetings

During those days every meeting with a friend or a relative who suddenly appeared from nowhere was a great and exciting surprise. There were those who had disappeared when the war began, and there were others whom I had left behind in the Ghetto and whose destiny was unknown to me. Here I would like to recall some surprising meetings which took place.

One day I was walking in the street, when a tall man with a long black beard, dressed shabbily, came towards me. At first I did not recognize him, but after a few seconds we hugged each other. The man was my cousin Yitskhak Hilelson, about whom I have written before in the chapter on my life in the Ghetto. Some time later he got a job in a military hospital in Kovno and continued with it until he went to Berlin. After the war he returned to Kovno, re-married and in 1956 came to Israel, together with his wife, her parents and his son. Yitskhak and his wife Khaya nee Khazanovitz passed away several years ago.

Another time, walking on Freedom Avenue, I met my friend Ze'ev Pak. He was dressed in military uniform and at first I did not notice that he had an artificial eye. This was a very surprising meeting. It was as though he came straight from heaven. Ze'ev and I had been good friends, ever since the 6th grade in the High School in Mariampol. He lived in a suburb of the city and was very poor. His father was an alcoholic, rather rare in those days among Jews, and his mother worked as a housemaid, since there was no other alternative for her. He studied at the High School, tuition free. I did not know and did not ask who supported him. We finished High School together and afterwards studied together at the Engineering Faculty of Kovno University, meeting often. When the war began he disappeared and I did not know what had happened to him. And now after three and a half years, I met him in the street. He told me that in the house he had lived in, his neighbors were families of Russian officers, then serving in Kovno. On the first or second day of the war, a truck arrived and took those families to Russia. He did not think twice, asked to join them and they agreed. So he came to Russia, where later on he was conscripted into the Lithuanian Division of the Red Army, wounded and lost an eye. As a disabled ex-serviceman he was accepted into the Plekhanov School of Economics and afterwards became chief of the Hebrew division in the Lenin library of Moscow. I received regards from him several times via Israeli researchers who visited that library, before he passed away a few years ago.

My cousin Gershon Hilelson and his wife arrived in Kovno at the beginning of the winter in 1945. The three men of the Hilelson family, Yitskhak, Aryeh and Gershon, had worked there before the war, and as previously discussed, only Yitzchak had spent time in the Kovno Ghetto. What had happened to the others I did not know. At the time when Gershon arrived in Kovno I thought that I would not stay in Kovno for long, so I let my room to them. Gershon's story was that when war began, he and his brother Aryeh with his wife managed to escape to Russia by train. He and Aryeh were called up into the Lithuanian Division, Aryeh was killed in battle and Gershon was wounded in the leg and became disabled. After he was demobilized, he married Aryeh's widow Tsilah. They lived in this flat in Kovno with their twins, Fania and Mosheh, until their immigration to Israel at the beginning of the 1970's. Later the whole family immigrated to Montreal, Canada, where Gershon and Tsilah died several years ago.

Masha Rabinovitz *(died in Israel)* married her pre-war friend Eliezer Aizenbud *(later professor)*, who managed to escape to Russia. They lived in that flat for years. She also had two children, who grew up together with Gershon's twins, and they remain close friends.

As told in previous chapters, I had a warm relationship with the Landau family in whose flat I lived as a student in Kovno. This relationship also continued in the Ghetto. There were three children in this family: daughter, son and daughter. One day my friend Peretz Kliachko came to tell me that he had met Malkah in the street helpless and crying, Malkah being the youngest daughter of the Landaus, now 12 or 13 years old. The Lithuanians who had hidden her in the country for some time, brought her to Kovno, and had simply abandoned her in the streets. She had no family left in Kovno, so I thought it best to bring her to the Dushauskas, as it seemed to me that she had been hidden in the country with their help. The Dushauskas family welcomed her with kindness and she stayed with them. They had one son the same age as Malkah.

Later I became aware that her sister, Miriam, who had also been hidden in a village, had returned to Kovno, but she became mentally ill and was hospitalized in a mental hospital.

Before leaving Kovno, I visited Mr. Dushauskas and told him my plan. He promised to adopt Malkah, which he did. I know that she finished High School and studied Engineering at the University. She married a Lithuanian man and had children. She became well known after establishing a plant in Mariampol. She died at aged 50. Later I found out that her father and brother had survived in the Dachau concentration camp and immigrated to America. If I had known then, in Kovno, all the events that were to occur on my way to Eretz-Yisrael, I would certainly have taken Malkah with me. But when I left Lithuania I had no idea what would happen to me on the way, and I was afraid to be responsible for the life of a 13 year old girl. I had virtually no money, and there was still a war going on in Europe. Later I regretted that I had left her in Kovno, and for years my conscience tormented me. I tried to contact her family in America, but did not succeed.

Several years ago my friend Professor Dov Levin told me that during a speech at a memorial assembly of Lithuanian Jewry in New York, he mentioned my name in connection with the publishing of the "Pinkas HaKehilot-Lita" by Yad Vashem. After the speech a man approached him saying that his name was David Landau and that I had lived with them in Kovno. I received his address in New Jersey, wrote him a letter and sent him my Memoirs in English. Some time later I received a recorded message from him, saying that he had tried to connect with me, but in the end there was no follow up.

Chapter 9: On My Way to *Eretz-Yisrael* (March 23, 1945-October 25, 1945)

Those Jewish youths who had a Zionist background understood that their future in the Soviet Union was doubtful. Having experienced Soviet rule in 1940-41, when the great Hebrew education network was liquidated and Zionist activity forbidden, it became clear that it was important to look for a way to leave Lithuania. The war was still going on then and in the liberated part of Eastern Europe there was much chaos. The idea was to take advantage of this situation and send people to look for a way to Eretz-Yisrael. There were rumors that it was possible to sail by ship from Romania to Eretz-Yisrael. The center of this activity was in Vilna, headed by Aba Kovner and two girls, all ex-partisans and ex-members of "HaShomer-Hatsair." One of those girls, Ruzhka Korchak, visited Kovno in November 1944 and met previous members of "HaShomer-HaTsair" in that city. Her task was to organize them into an Underground movement, whose job it would be to take out its members from Lithuania to Eretz-Yisrael. Indeed, the initiative originated in this organization, but immediately all the other Ex-Zionist youth organizations joined, and thus the so called "Coordination" was established.

In order to travel from one city to another in those days, one had to get a document called "Komandirovka" from one's working place, which stated the destination, the aim of the journey, etc. One also had to have a certificate confirming that the traveler was really an employee of the firm which issued this "Komandirovka."

Only with those documents was it possible to buy a ticket for the train, which was then the only means of transportation that was functioning. In brief, travelling was not simple then, and friends, who were employed in the Lithuanian Prime Minister's office or in the Building Trust, issued such documents for members of the underground who had to travel. Only the forms were original, all the other items, such as stamps, were forged by specialists.

In November 1944 two people were sent from Vilna to Romania in order to check the possibility of sailing from there to Eretz-Yisrael. The two were Ruzhka Korchak and Dr. Amerant *(He was a teacher at the Hebrew Teachers Seminar in Vilna and later at the Seminar in Haifa. He has since passed away).* One of them had to stay in Romania to organize a base for the groups about to come, whereas the other had to return to Vilna to report on the trip and the possibilities. To cross the border between the Soviet Union and a neighboring country in those days was difficult and dangerous. Nevertheless, with the help of Jews they met on their way they managed to arrive in Romania, where they met two men from Eretz-Yisrael, who were busy organizing legal and illegal "Aliyah." A ship was getting ready to sail with legal immigrants from the port of Konstanza by the Black Sea to Eretz- Yisrael. It so happened that some woman gave up her "Certificate" and the "Aliyah" delegates convinced Ruzhka, after they had heard her stories, to join this ship. Thus she arrived in Eretz-Yisrael on the December 12, 1944 and was the first person to tell her own shocking experience to the public in Israel. She described what had happened to Lithuanian Jewry during Nazi rule. She wrote her memoirs of this period in the book "Lehavoth BaEifer" *(Flames in Ashes)*. She was a member of the editorial board of the periodical "Moreshet." She died several years ago while living in Kibbutz Ein HaKhoresh.

Dr. Amerant returned to Vilna and slowly groups began to move towards Romania. Sometimes mistakes were made, as a result of which people were arrested and imprisoned for months, until the Organization managed to free them. This was the beginning of the "Brikha" *(Escape)* Organization, which later on included thousands from all over Europe, whose aim it was to reach Eretz-Yisrael.

"Repatriation" to Poland

Our main problem was how to cross the border between the Soviet Union and Poland. From there it was not so clear how to move further on to Romania, but we believed that it would be much easier. At that time, the repatriation agreement between the Soviet Union and Poland was published, stating that all Polish citizens, who were in the Soviet Union during the war, could return to their homeland. This agreement also applied to the Vilna region, which until 1940 was under Polish rule. Anyone who could prove by some document that he was a Polish citizen was allowed to return. Our organization decided to use this agreement. In the town of Lida, which until 1940 belonged to Poland, but now to Belarus, our people found a Russian officer who worked in the Office for Internal Affairs. For substantially large payments, he issued birth certificates for Jews who were born in Lida and had disappeared in the "Holocaust." As the Organization had no money, anyone who wanted to get such a certificate had to pay a few hundred rubles for it, however it should be truthfully noted that not one of the members of the Organization was left behind in Lithuania because of lack of money. I had to find a sum of money which was more than twice my monthly salary. I recalled the two items Yakov Gidansky had hidden with Engineer Mackevicius's family (see above). I found his address, went there, introduced myself as Yakov's cousin and asked for the two items which Yakov had given him for safekeeping. I told him that I did not know at that moment where Yakov was and if any member of his family returned, I would settle accounts with him. He and his wife asked me to come back the next day, when they gave me the golden chain and the ring. I sold the chain, enabling me to pay for the birth certificate and even getting an additional few hundred rubles for myself, but I kept the ring. Now is the time to tell what happened to me later as a result of these items.

With the liquidation of the Kovno Ghetto, Yakov and his wife were sent to Germany: she to Stutthof where she perished, and he to Dachau where he survived, this time also thanks to his being a vulcanization specialist. After liberation from the camp, he decided to return to Lithuania, believing in the illusion that his wife had also survived and might return to Kovno. In Kovno he got his old job back in the factory for rubber products, together with Mackevicius, who told him that he had given me the two trinkets. I sold the ring in Alba-Julia (Transilvania), as will be told later, for which I bought a black woolen suit and had some remaining money.

After renewing my connection with Yakov in Kovno, I sent him that suit as well as some other things he asked for, blades, for example. I think I also sent him another parcel, but I was a student then at the Technion and had no money. Parcels to the Soviet Union cost a lot of money, because it was obligatory to pay the Soviet custom fees here in Israel. During the dark years of Stalin's rule the connection between me and Ya'akov was cut off. Some years later Yakov's sister, Paula, who lived in the USA, visited Israel and I met her at their Uncle Yitskhak Kubovitzky's house in Tel Aviv. She asked me, on behalf of Ya'akov, for a big sum of money for the two trinkets, their size and value having increased in Ya'akov's imagination over time. I told her that I would settle accounts with Ya'akov when I met him and indeed, when he arrived in Israel in the 1970's, I invited him to our flat. We discussed the matter and I gave him money to buy a refrigerator. So this matter, which on the one hand helped me to leave Lithuania but on the other caused me some embarrassment, was finally resolved. Kubovitzky, whose wife was my Mother's and Barukh's cousin, told my Uncle Barukh what had happened, and I had to justify my actions to him.

I now return to my story. I paid the required sum for the birth certificate and waited for the call to move. The problem of how to get a "Komandirovka" for travelling from Kovno to Vilna, from the office where Yonah and I worked now became an issue. We decided to steal the forms from the manpower chief's office. In our office there were turns of duty at night, and one of the employees had to stay in the office after working hours until the next morning. One night, when Yonah was on duty, I hid until all the employees had left the office.

During that night we managed to get into the office of the manpower chief and steal the necessary forms.

To fill out these forms and to affix the round stamp, *(in the USSR a document without a round stamp looked in the eyes of even low level officials as not valid enough)*, without which the forms were useless, was the concern of the specialists in the Underground.

With these documents we arrived in Vilna, where we stayed overnight with a Jewish family, and the next day traveled by train to Grodno, a city near the Polish border. In Grodno we burned all our documents and received new identities as repatriates. According to the documents we bought, we now became a family named "Hustig," I being its head. To make a convincing impression, I grew a mustache. My so called wife was Rachel Zagai (now in Lehavot HaBashan), my son was Yonah Rochman, who put on shorts, and there were more members of that family, whom I have meanwhile forgotten. One of them was the daughter of a prominent doctor in Kovno who later married the well known Prof. Ezra Zohar. She recently passed away.

Travelling through Poland

That evening we entered the train which took us to Poland, arriving in Bialystok (Poland) the next morning, after crossing the border without any problems. This was on March 23rd or March 24th 1945. From Bialystok we traveled to Lublin, where activity for leaving Poland in the direction of Eretz-Yisrael was centered. It is worthwhile mentioning that the war in Europe was still going on. Transportation in Poland was operational mainly for the Red Army civilians. People like us had to find different means of travelling from one place to another. Indeed we traveled in cattle wagons, on the coal trailer of the locomotive, in carts, and walked a lot by foot.

In Lublin a group of ex-members of the Zionist youth organizations from Poland and Lithuania who had spent the war in Russia, had arrived, by legal or illegal ways and means. Lublin was then the temporary capital of the Polish Government, established with the encouragement of the Soviets. There were arguments among and between the activists of the "Bricha," as well as those close to the government, as to whether to act illegally and so offend the new government, or to wait until law and order was established and then leave Poland legally. This argument was won by the supporters of the first alternative, and in hindsight it must be said that they were right.

We arrived in Lublin and after staying there for a few days, joined up with a group composed of ex-members of "HaShomer HaTsair," whose leader was appointed. Forged documents from the Red Cross were deposited in his hands for each member of the group with Yugoslavian and Greek names. These documents had to be used in order to cross the border between Poland and Czechoslovakia and further on through Hungary to Romania. Our alibi, in case of questioning, was that we were returning to our homeland after having been freed from forced labor in Germany. Inside Poland we had certificates from the Red Cross, stating that we were Polish citizens looking for our families. The leader of the group had also received a sum of money for our expenses for our way and travel.

In order to alleviate difficulties for the travelers, transit points on the escape

(Brikhah) route were established. In these places Underground activists would welcome the travelers, feed them, provide accommodation and give advice for the journey to come. Such stations were established in cities of south eastern Poland not far from the Czechoslovakian border, such as Zseshuv, Krosno, Sanok etc.

I do not remember all the details of that trip anymore, but I do want to describe one event. One day we waited at some junction for a lift to Zheshuv, where we wanted to go to the transit station there. It was before dusk and a military truck from the Polish (Red) Army stopped, an officer with a square topped cap looked at the people waiting, among whom there were also Poles, and he asked silently "amkha?" (in Hebrew your-God's- people). When he heard that we were indeed "amkha" (Jewish) he allowed us to climb on his truck and he took us to Zseshuv. We were not aware of the dangers awaiting Jews on the roads of Poland, as anti-Semitism among the Poles did not subside, on the contrary, it increased! In every Jew who returned to his village from a concentration camp or from the Soviet Union, they saw someone dangerous to themselves. They were afraid they would have to return property they had stolen from their Jewish neighbors, and may also have been frightened of possible revenge.

In the city of Kielze, the Poles killed 41 Jews who had gathered there, among them the only survivors of families who had been murdered. There were other cases, where single Jews were murdered when returning to their home villages.

We arrived at Zheshuv and looked for the address of Rabbi Dr. Toren. On finally arriving there I got a surprise, the door was opened by a young woman who had been with us in the Underground in the Kovno Ghetto. She had been hidden in a village with the help of the Lithuanian Priest, as told in the previous chapter.

Meanwhile she had married Dr. Toren, who was the Chief Rabbi of the Polish Army and had a high military rank. In fact this flat was used only as camouflage, whereas the real transit station was the flat next door.

There I got another surprise, when I found that my friend from the "Partizanka" and from the army, Yitskhak Kuperberg and his wife Tsiporah, ran this station *(both have died in Israel)*. The joy of these surprises and meetings was great. We slept there for one night and the next day went on to Krosno, the next transit point, where we became Yugoslavians and Greeks. Here our appearance was checked and changed, in order not to be too well dressed and to appear just like poor refugees from labor camps in Germany.

The trip from there to Romania in fact Transilvania, lasted a week. On our way we passed Slovakia and the north eastern corner of Hungary. In the Slovakian town of Humene, there was another transit station, but I do not remember details. When we were among strangers, on trains for example, we spoke to each other in Hebrew or Lithuanian, two strange languages in those countries. What the Lithuanian and Greek languages have in common are only the '-is' and '-as' at the end of nouns and family names. Occasionally there were confusing situations due to our charade. In one town, in a house where refugees were being cared for, a hostess told us that a high officer of the Tito Partisans was staying in town and that she had sent for him, as we would surely be happy to meet a fellow citizen. And indeed a uniformed man appeared, looking for his fellow citizens. We said that we were sorry, but the Yugoslavians among us had gone to the city for a walk, and only the Greeks were here.

In Romania

And so we travelled from one place to another until we arrived in Romania. The first town we arrived in was Oradea-Mare, where we stayed in a house, which had formerly been a Jewish school. From there we travelled to Kluj, where we stayed for a few days. Here we met more groups from Lithuania and from Poland, among them the group which included Peninah, my future wife. Peninah, nee Cypkiewitz, was from Wloclawek *(Poland)*. She and her two friends, Rachel Beker *(Tratsevitzky)* and Halina Shmulevitz *(Barkani)* came from Chenstokhova, where they were liberated by the Red Army from the "Hassag" camp, a German ammunitions factory, in January, 1945. Peninah and Rachel were members of "HaShomer HaTsair" and of the Underground and it was not difficult for them to make contact with the "Brikha" organization. After many adventures they, together with Halina, arrived in Alba-Julia, a small town in Transilvania, where our group was also sent.

Until then all the "refugees" had been sent to Bucarest, but when all the rooms in this city were occupied, the potential "Olim" were sent to other cities. Alba-Julia had a famous church, where the kings of Romania were crowned. In this town we were surprised to find a Jewish population, which had been able to keep its stores throughout the war. Actually there were no young Jewish men in the town, but there had not been total extermination, as compared to Lithuania or Poland.

The place that had been rented for us was a square yard, with a high wooden gate and a wicket for pedestrians on one side of it. On the other side there stood one-story buildings. In one of them there was a kitchen, and there was also a small building which was probably the office, the two main buildings having a veranda with entrances leading to the rooms. Later we realized that this place had been a brothel, belonging to a local Jew from whom we had rented it. He sometimes came to us and, according to rumors, said that, with God's help, he would open his business again.

Every room had bunk beds, which accommodated 8-10 people, and daily life was organized like in a Kibbutz. There was a secretariat which maintained contact with the center in Bucarest, which also supplied the funds for our daily upkeep.

At one time we received clothes, apparently from the "Joint" ("Joint Distribution Committee," an international organization helping Jewish people all over the world), which were distributed among us.

In addition to the secretariat, there were several elected committees, such as the economic or cultural or work committees etc. The types of work to be performed consisted of turns of duty in the kitchen and dining room, as well as cleaning the premises. Apart from these activities there was nothing to do.

With a group of friends in Alba-Julia, June 1945

Standing from left: ----, Peninah, I ,----, Halina Shmulevitz, Khanah Rokhman, Yonah Rokhman *, Rachel Beker, David Rubinshtein *, -----, -----.

Sitting from left: Grisha Shefer, Bolek Gevirtsman *, Leizer Ludovsky *, Yitskhak Vidokle, Ze'ev Gedud, -----.

Sitting on the floor: Pola Beker, Pola Rapaport *, Mosheh Zinger, Zelda *,-----.

(*) passed away

Peninah and Josef at our wedding, Alba Julia, May 1945

The Wedding Party

We arrived in Alba-Julia at the end of April 1945. It was spring and in our "Kibbutz" there were many young people, boys and girls, who had lost all their families and remained alone. The absence of worry for the future and the illusion that the world would be a better place now, made love flourish and encourage couples, like Peninah and myself.

Peninah *(she was called Pola at home)* lived with her Father Eliezer, Mother Gitel and brother Shemuel in Wloclawek, a town about 150 km north-west of Warsaw on the shore of the Wisla River, till WWII.

What happened to her and her family during the terrible times and how she and her brother survived, is told in her book "Chapters in my Life," Haifa 1996.

Peninah was a beautiful and lovely girl, feminine, with two dimples in her cheeks and a very nice voice, a sports woman, full of animation and falling in love was mutual. Often we would go uphill to the Church, sit in the meadow, talk to each other about the past and sometimes even run around the meadow. The language common to both of us was Yiddish, which was not strange Peninah, but after five years of war, she had somewhat forgotten it. After a short time the two of us moved closer to each other, as we had much in common and we liked to walk. One evening on guard duty together at the gate, we decided to spend our lives together.

On May 25, 1945, after a friendship of about five weeks, Peninah and I married. It was a wedding without a Rabbi, because it was strictly forbidden to tell even the local Jews that I came from Lithuania. For security reasons the "Lithuanian" group posed as refugees from Poland. Romania was then under Soviet Rule, and if the authorities had known the truth they could have sent them back to Lithuania and this, of course, was very dangerous for them. Only later in Eretz-Yisrael were we married according to Jewish law. But our friends in the Kibbutz in Alba-Julia made a great wedding party for us. Arranging many tables together in the yard, they made one long table covered with white sheets. Meir Tratsevitsky, who was a member of the secretariat and his friend Ephrayim, who was in charge of provisions, generously prepared refreshments and drinks. Everything went off in a joyful atmosphere, until someone poured spirit into the wine and many people got drunk, among them Halina. The next morning she didn't remember how she had managed to get to her room and how it had happened that her glasses were found in the lavatory.

On May 9th we celebrated the end of the war. A victory parade took place in the town in which many local organizations participated and we included. After the parade there was a party in the Kibbutz and in addition to me there were two more fellows who played music: one on the accordion and the other a trumpet.

I played all the popular Russian and other songs well and was welcomed in every party and was also elected to the cultural committee.

The good life in Alba-Julia continued as before. We were very eager for amusements, probably in order to compensate for the lost years in the Nazi inferno. Even the smallest event, like getting a dress from the "Joint," a birthday etc., was reason for celebrating. We also celebrated Peninah's birthday on June 15th in Alba-Julia, when I presented her with material for a gown which we had both selected. It was a nice flowery cloth suitable for her suntanned face and a local dressmaker sewed the dress for her. I had some money from a ring (as told before in page 124) I had sold to a local Jew and thanks to the money we had, we went to a guest performance of an opera which took place in a cinema in the town. It was very crowded and very hot, and neither of us remembers the name of the opera we saw.

Other couples who began their future relationship in this "Kibbutz" were Grisha and Zlatka, now in Eilon, Rachel and Meir, now in Nir David, Nekhamah and Yitskhak, now in Kefar Masarik, and many more. There were also a few married couples, such as Yonah and Khanah Rokhman, David and Rachel Levin and others.

A group of friends on the occasion of our wedding, Alba-Julia, May 1945

Standing from right: Efraim-----, Meir Tratsevitsky, Rachel Beker, Halina Shmulevitz, David Rubinstein, Misha Soltz

Sitting from right: Pola Beker, Josef and Peninah, Grisha Shefer

At our Golden Wedding Anniversary, Haifa, May 1995

Standing from right: Meir Tratsevitsky, Rachel Beker-Tratsevitsky, Halina Shmulevitz-Barkani,

Sitting from right: Josef, Peninah, Grisha Shefer

There was a young disabled Jewish fellow in town, who hardly walked, even with the help of two sticks. He visited us frequently and kept inviting us, i.e .Halina, Peninah, Rachel, Meir and me, to a pub *("Bodega"),* where we would drink sparkling Romanian wine. He had money, something we did not have, so we willingly accepted his invitations. On one of these occasions he asked me in a whisper how to say in Polish: "I love you" in order to say this to Halina. Since I did not know any Polish, I could not help him and so a very unpleasant situation developed. I avoided answering him, which he took to mean that I was jealous, to which again I did not react. This incident chilled relations between us a little.

Usually we looked for any reason whatever to celebrate in a "Bodega," such as when Meir got a suit from the "Joint" or somebody had a birthday, any reason was good enough to go to a "Bodega" and drink wine.

My friend Khayim Galin, who arrived to Transilvania in the same way, was sent with a group to the town Turda. Hearing that I married, he came to Alba-Julia to congratulate me and Peninah, whom he had never met. On this occasion we, the three partisans of the same regiment, were photographed.

This good life continued till the middle of June. At that time a large contingent of soldiers of the Red Army arrived in town, apparently for a rest. Looking for girls, they were directed to our place, because of its known past as a house of prostitution.

We were forced to post a guard at the gate, and when Russian soldiers approached he would signal, whereupon the girls had to disappear into the rooms. The soldiers were told that there were no girls here and that this was not the same institution that had been there before. One day two or three Russian officers, a little drunk, came to the gate and wanted to get in. The signal was given and all the girls disappeared. Only Esther R., a nice blond girl remained on the veranda. When the officers saw her, they pushed their way into the yard, but a few of our strong men, ex Partisans, prevented their advance. One of the Russian officers took out a small caliber pistol, shot and wounded one of our boys slightly.

High military police officers arrived to investigate the incident, questioning us as to who we were and what were we doing there. I do not know if this event was what determined our departure from Romania, or whether the Organization had in any case given up the idea of illegal Aliya from this state.

Through Hungary and Austria to Italy

During these days, delegates from the Jewish Brigade, then stationed in Italy, arrived in Bucarest, and after some time it was decided to transfer all potential "Olim" to Italy. One part of our Kibbutz made the trip to Italy through Yugoslavia, whereas the others went through Hungary and Austria, among them Peninah and I. We traveled up to the Hungarian border by train as Polish refugees, who were ostensibly returning to their homeland. At the border we were furnished with forged documents of Austrian Jews, on their way home to Austria, and thus we arrived at the local transit station in Budapest. We stayed in this city for a few days and met other Lithuanian Jews there, who had been freed from the Dachau Concentration Camp. Exciting meetings took place between members of families who had been separated, such as when one member had hidden during the liquidation of the Ghetto or had joined the Partisans, and the other one was sent to Dachau and managed to survive.

Hungary and Austria were, from the Russian viewpoint, enemy states and the soldiers behaved towards the people of those states accordingly. From Budapest we had to travel to Graz in Austria, where we were to cross the border between the Russian and British occupation zones, and then travel on to Italy. At the railway station in Budapest we noticed that every train compartment was occupied by one or two Russian officers, who did not allow anybody else to enter them. We also saw that the local population traveled by sitting on the roofs of the railway carriages, so having no choice, we did the same, travelling like this all the way to Graz. We were lucky that it did not rain during the 36-hour journey on the roof. It was amusing to see the conductor climbing onto the roof in order to perforate the tickets. As refugees with "documents" of the Red Cross, we were allowed to travel without tickets.

In retrospect I would say that this journey was a very dangerous adventure, due to the tunnels and the electric wires which crossed the tracks. When nearing obstacles, somebody would shout "heads," and we would quickly lie down instead of sitting up. Falling asleep was also very dangerous, but we looked after one another and except for a few items which were blown off the roof, we arrived in Graz safely. In Graz we were put up in Hotel Weizner, another transit point of the "Brikha."

This hotel was the height of luxury, every couple being allotted a separate room, white-coated waiters moving around in the dining room, the tables were covered with white tablecloths and many plates and cutlery, but food was sparse. We stayed in this hotel only one day, and continued our journey the next day, but only after we had handed over the watches which some of us still had. These watches were used to bribe the Russian soldiers at a specific point on the border, where we would be crossing into the British zone. In order not to cause too much attention, we were instructed to go in pairs and to keep visual contact with each other. One pair who knew the way walked ahead, the others followed. We proceeded on a path through beautiful woods, crossed the border and waited for the pairs behind us, but they did not arrive. I do not remember anymore whether they arrived eventually on the same day or the day after. The reason they did not arrive together with us was due to our friend, Halina. She had walked along with some fellow, and at one point, where the path split into two directions, did not pay attention, and instead of going left as required, she and her escort went straight ahead, where they and all the pairs behind them walked directly into the guards' hut. There they were detained but, as everything had been organized beforehand, were released after a short time.

We had been instructed to go to a Refugee Camp, which the British Army had established near the town of Villach, where we received food and a place to sleep. After a few days we were told that if we wanted to stay there for a longer period, we would have to work in the nearby mines. A British armed soldier was stationed at the camp gate and the situation became complicated.

Meeting the Jewish Brigade and the Camp in Tervisio

One day we were told to sneak out of the camp, one by one, each one with his parcel of belongings, and to meet up with the others at some point along the road. On arrival, we saw several military tarpaulin covered trucks standing there, and on their tail boards the emblem of the Jewish Brigade: two blue stripes between a white one and on it the yellow Star of David. The drivers wore British uniforms and their sleeves sported the same emblem. Today it is difficult to describe the experience of this meeting with soldiers from Eretz-Yisrael. The surprise was great, as if angels had come down to us from heaven. The sight of the emblems of the Brigade on the trucks and on the soldiers' sleeves was the compensation we now received for all the humiliation and troubles we had experienced until now. We felt indescribably happy.

After emotions had subsided, we climbed onto the trucks and started to move. At a certain check point the trucks stopped, we sat quietly and waited as to see what would happen next. Soon the back curtain of the truck was raised, a soldier put his head into the truck and asked in Hebrew: "Is there someone here from Lodz?" The soldiers from Eretz-Yisrael were searching among the masses of refugees who were now streaming to Italy, for relatives and friends who might have survived.

We continued to travel until we arrived at a big transit camp near Tervisio, which the Brigade had established with the help of the Jewish authorities in Eretz-Yisrael. This was the "Center for the Diaspora" (Merkaz Lagola) headed by enlisted personalities from Eretz-Yisrael (M.Surkis etc). Exciting meetings took place in this camp between friends from the past and even between parents and brothers, where one part of the family had come from Eretz- Yisrael as soldiers and the other part from the death camps. In our group there were the two brothers Sandovski from Piotrkov in Poland, who, here in Tervisio, met two other brothers, who had come as soldiers from Eretz- Yisrael. Yitskhak and Shulamith Rabinovitz and their young son from Kovno, freed from Dachau and Stutthof, met two other sons, soldiers in the Brigade. There were many such exciting meetings in this camp.

The soldiers pampered us, giving us almost everything they had, such as cigarettes, chocolate, uniforms etc, etc. It is important to recall that in those days in Italy one could get anything one wanted in exchange for cigarettes or chocolate. Peninah's friend, Rachel Beker, met soldiers who had been her friends in "HaShomer HaTsair" in Warsaw. The week or so we were in Tervisio we spent together with them and felt as though messianic times had come. Together we made trips into the mountains, and in the evenings enjoyed performances by actors from Eretz-Yisrael. Meeting up with soldiers of the Brigade and those days in Tervisio became deeply engraved in our minds, and many years later we would recall this episode when with our friends, with much affection and gratitude. It was the greatest excitement I had experienced in those years. The efforts the Brigade and other Jewish units in the British army in Italy made for the refugees, who were wandering on the roads of Europe, some of them without any clear aim as regards the future have been documented in many books and this is not the place to go into particulars. But from my own experience I can verify that the moral help and support I got from the actual fact of their appearance, was enormous. For us they symbolized the Land (Eretz-Yisrael) and the future.

Italy and the "Dror" Camp

Here in Tervisio the Center organized a group of some tens of young men and women, mostly ex-members of the Zionist youth organizations, and sent this group to a camp of the Royal Engineers in Mestre near Venice. This happened on July 22, 1945.

This unit, its number was 738, was composed only of Jewish officers and soldiers from Eretz-Yisrael. Here we were stayed in a big hall on the second floor of a building, the entrance to which was from the same yard as that of the lodgings of the soldiers. We slept in collapsible military beds, each of them covered with mosquito netting because of the many mosquitoes which originated in the smelly canal nearby. We wore military shirts we received from the soldiers and all our needs were looked after by them. One of the soldiers there had the job of caring for all our needs, on behalf of the "Merkaz Lagola." To the outside we appeared as civilian laborers who were helping the unit to fulfill its assignments, which actually were very few. I remember that we went a few times to repair the lighting installations at the port of Venice. We would leave the camp at about 8:00 am, travel half an hour to the port, work till 9:30am, then travel back to the camp for tea. We were back to the port by 11:00 am and at 12:00 pm travel back to the camp for lunch. The 10:00 am tea was a sacred institution in the British Army and I wondered how it functioned at the front in battle.

Penina, Josef and Yona Rokhman in Venice, 1945

Mestre

Peninah (fourth from the left) and
Josef (second from the left) on a
military truck

From left: Raya Zilberfarb, Khayim
Yaskulka Peninah, Yisrael Gringer,
Halina Shmulevitz

Sitting: Sima------, Pola Rapaport

Daily life in our group was organized just like a Kibbutz. Many committees were elected to deal with current concerns. I was elected to the cultural committee, whose duty it was to plan the "Oneg Shabbath" parties etc. Various types of workshops existed in the camp and the soldiers were ready to teach anyone who showed an interest in basic trades, such as the work of a locksmith, for example.

It was from this camp that I wrote a letter to my Uncle in Tel Aviv, after not having written for five months because of circumstances, and in it I told him, among other things, about my connection with Peninah. One day, a soldier from the Brigade (*Israel Gringer*) appeared in our camp, an ex-member of "HaShomer HaTsair" in Warsaw, and invited Peninah and Halina for a trip to Venice. I did not join them, because I was busy in the cultural committee. In Venice they wanted to sail in a gondola, but instead of going down the steps and into the gondola, they jumped from the quay right into it. First Israel jumped, then Peninah, but she fell into the water instead, and as she did not know how to swim, Israel and the gondolist jumped into the water and pulled her out, all wet. The gondolist felt guilty and sailed with them for hours in order to get her dry, at the end taking them to his flat where Peninah ironed her dress.

The day did not end with this adventure. That night, after having spent the day in Venice, they made their way back to Mestre. There in the street, a few Italian men attacked them and wanted to cut

Peninah's hair, thinking she was an Italian girl going out with a British soldier. Israel fought with them, losing two of his front teeth in the turmoil. Peninah did not know what the Italians wanted from her, and thought that they intended to slaughter her with their knives because she was Jewish. They succeeded in cutting only a small curl of her hair. Israel Gringer became a member of Kibbutz Lehavot Habashan later on, left the Kibbutz, married, and died of a heart attack when he was only 33 years old.

Our stay in Mestre remained a pleasant memory for us. We had no concerns, went on trips with the soldiers to Venice and other places and arranged parties, and so the time passed. Several girls of our group married soldiers they met in this camp, later on after their arrival in Israel.

After about a month in this camp, a situation developed, which forced our beneficiary unit to evacuate us. British high ranking officers started to pay too much attention to our group. So we were transferred to a village (I have forgotten its name) where a nice house was rented for us. We were joined by another group of youths, all from Poland. In this place we stayed for a month, until some of us, mainly ex-members of "HaShomer HaTsair," were ordered to move southwards to Bari. We were taken to a railway station, and found it extremely difficult to get onto the train to Rome. At midnight we arrived at a station, where we had to change trains for Bari. We found the correct train, but it was full to capacity, all the compartments and passages being filled with people and parcels, and it seemed impossible to get inside. And then something happened, which caused us to appreciate the Italian people. They started to pull us up into the train, one by one, and at the end all of us were inside, and together with them, standing like sardines in a can. Sometimes it was more convenient to stand on one foot only, because there was no room for the other one. In this manner we traveled throughout the night, the train was dark and all the passengers stood and sang Italian songs. It was an unforgettable experience.

Illegal Aliya (Ha'apala)

We arrived in Bari at dawn and went to a certain address, where we waited until military trucks came and took us to a remote place, amid vineyards. A transit camp for potential "Olim" named "Dror"

(Freedom), had been established here, consisting of a few barracks and some service buildings. Peninah and I received a very small space and there we settled down. Apparently it had been a camping site or something similar. The camp was a long way from a highway and in order to reach it we had to travel for many km. through vineyards and olive groves. By the way, this was the first time I saw olives and I tried eating them straight from the tree. They were very bitter of course, and I spat them out. In the camp we passed the time, among other things, by teaching Hebrew to those who did not know the language and the "Litvaks" among us, the graduates of the Hebrew high schools, were the teachers. We arranged "Oneg Shabbath" parties with different programs and I took an important part in them. Here, too, my harmonica was the only musical instrument. The administrators of the camp were several soldiers from Eretz-Yisrael, nominated by the "Merkaz Lagolah." The food there was very sparse, but except for this, time passed by pleasantly. In the camp we received Hebrew newspapers from Eretz-Yisrael. One day, it was after Rosh Hashanah (1945), I read in the newspaper "Davar" that the ship "Transilvania" had arrived in Eretz-Yisrael, and on it a large number of legal "Olim", survivors of the Holocaust, among them the active Zionist worker from Kovno, Eliezer Rozentsvaig and his son Zerubavel. Rachel Rosentzvaig-Levin was with us in "Dror" and had no idea what had happened to her family. She had escaped from the transport of the Ghetto inhabitants when they were sent to Germany after the liquidation of the Ghetto. During the few weeks until the liberation of Kovno by the Red Army, she hid with Lithuanians, but her father, her mother and her brother were sent to Germany. Now I had the privilege of informing her that her father and brother had survived and that they were already in Eretz-Yisrael.

In "Dror" we stayed for about a month, and on the night of October 15, 1945 were taken by covered military trucks to a small port near Bari. Previously we had been told not to take any parcels, and specifically no documents and pictures which could identify us. Peninah and I handed our few pictures to a soldier. Fortunately we received these pictures later on once we were in *Eretz-Yisrael,* but many others lost everything. At the port we were transferred into small boats that took us to the ship. I remember that when we embarked I thought that this small ship would convey us to the real ship, the one in which we would be sailing to *Eretz-Yisrael.* But I soon realized our mistake, and it was indeed this small ship that took us to our planned destination. It was an Italian fishing vessel named "Petro."

A four story wooden contraption had been erected in its hold, with sheets of tarpaulin tied between its planks, so that there was a space of about 40-50 cm width and of similar height for everyone to lie on. Such an installation can be seen at the "Museum of the Ha'apala (Illegal Aliyah)" in Haifa, where the ship "*Af Al Pi"(*)* is on display. In this manner 180 people were crowded into this ship, in addition to the crew. The captain was an Italian and with him a "Palyam"(**) commander. There was also an escort from the authorities in Eretz-Yisrael, an Israeli radio operator and a few Italian sailors. Most of the time was spent in the holds below, as we were not allowed to climb on deck, in order not to be discovered by British planes.

Only at night people climbed on deck to breathe fresh air, but many were seasick and did not want to leave their beds. Inside the holds it was very warm, and the air stank, because many people vomited. Penina, Khana and Lea got places near the opening, because they were already pregnant. Most of the people did not eat the meals which had been prepared for them. I was nominated to apportion drinking water, one bottle per day per person. I felt well and even had an appetite, but for the first time I saw how seasickness can transform healthy people into helpless ones. There was an ex-Partisan *(Barukh Levin)*, a sabotage expert, who had excelled in blowing up German trains and was rewarded for his exploits with the ensignia of the "Hero of the Soviet Union." It was a strange sight to see how his tiny wife carried him to the toilet. Near the island of Crete the sea became so stormy, that the big soup pot, when lifted to the deck, had to be secured tightly, so that it would not slip into the sea.

Thus we sailed for seven days, and on the eighth night came near the shores of the "Promised Land." Due to the late hour, it was impossible to disembark, so we were forced to sail along the coast all the next day, during which time all passengers had to stay below, in the holds. That night we approached the coast between Kibbutz Shefayim and Moshav Rishpon. Everyone went down into the boats, which took them fairly close to the shore and there, in order not to get their feet wet, the boys of the "Haganah" carried the people to dry land on their shoulders. This was done because we still had to walk a few km. on foot to previously designated places, and it was not convenient to do so with wet feet and trousers.

(*)"Nevertheless" the British' the Aliya will continue

(**) Palyam"-the navy unit of the "Palmach"-the Shock Troops of the "Haganah"

I will never forget the scented smell of the land, while walking eight kms. to Moshav Giv'at Chen. The young and the strong were sent to this Moshav, and the others to the rest home in Shefayim. Along our route, we saw armed boys of the "Haganah," whose job it was to protect the path we had to take, and this impressed us very much. In Giv'at Khen everybody was awake, despite the late hour. Every family took two boys to their house. Dov Levin and I were taken by the Fruchters, where we received a hot shower and a big supper. This was the first time I ate margarine and I thought it was butter. After supper and showering, we slipped into soft beds with white sheets, a strange feeling after not having slept like this for so long. When I closed my eyes, I felt that everything was rocking, as though we were still on board ship. Some of the boys told us in the morning, that they were not able to sleep in the beds, and lay on the floor instead. My friend Dov Levin has kept in touch with the Fruchters until now.

(On the 40th anniversary of our "Aliya" we arranged a meeting in Tel Aviv and this family was also invited. This meeting was attended by about 50 people, among them M.Surkis, who was the head of "Merkaz Lagola" in those days, as well as the Israeli captain of the ship and the Israeli escort, a member of Kibbutz Yagur. From the Fruchter family, the married daughter and her husband came along).

The next morning a bus arrived and took us, the ex members of "HaShomer HaTsair," to Kibbutz Ma'anith. Another group was taken to Kibbutz Ma'aleh HaKhamisha, others went to relatives or wherever they wanted. In Ma'anith there was a veteran group of members from the Lithuanian movement.

Exciting meetings took place between relatives and friends. Thus, for example, my friend Yonah Rochman met his brother Ya'akov, who had been a member of this Kibbutz from before the war.

After several days in Ma'anith, someone decided to transfer us to Kibbutz Beth Zera, the first Kibbutz of the movement in Lithuania. There, Peninah and I got a room in a barracks, which to us looked like a palace. Rachel Zagai joined us in this room as a "Primus" (*) as it was called. We got a warm welcome from the veteran members of that Kibbutz, Peninah and I being very warmly treated by Judith Borokhovitz-Yaron, who knew me and my family from Kibart. After four and a half years I was now able to eat until I was full. I still remember the big salads I prepared for myself in the dining room of the kibbutz and also the yeast cakes we ate for breakfast on Shabbath.

In the eyes of the British Authorities we were illegal immigrants, and could not go anywhere without some documents. Only after a few months did we receive identity cards. How this was accomplished, I do not know. After getting these cards, Peninah and I went to Tel Aviv to visit my Uncle Barukh and his family. He himself was at that time in the USA. In Tel Aviv I felt at home and had no absorption difficulties. The education I had received at home, at school and in the youth movement, contributed much to that feeling. For Peninah it was a little more difficult, because she did not know enough Hebrew at this time.

(*) A third person in a room of a couple. It was a necessity because of lack of space for everybody.

Beth-Zera

From left: ------, Mira Buz, Peninah, Josef, Khanah and Yonah Rokhman

From left: Pesakh Shemesh, Josef, Barukh Shub, Dov Levin, Avraham Anzel, Grisha Shefer

The above is the story of that part of my life, which ended with my "Aliya," a dream which had now turned into reality.

Postscript

On the 11th of May 1946 our son Amikam was born in Beth-Zera. In the autumn of that year we left the Kibbutz and moved to Haifa, with the aim of continuing my studies at the Civil Engineering Faculty of the Technion. I was accepted in the second course and after a further year's delay because of the War of Independence, I completed my studies in 1950 with the degree of Engineer. In 1958 I received my M.Sc. in Agricultural Engineering.

During the War of Independence I served in the Air Force in the Aerial Photography Unit and was discharged with the rank of Staff Sergeant. Until the age of 54 I served in the Army Reserves and during this time I contributed my modest part in the Sinai and Yom Kippur wars.

In 1967 I was granted the "Medal as a Fighter against the Nazis" by The Israeli Defense Ministry. (see my discharge certificate from the Army)

During the years 1950-1952 I worked for the Water Department of the Ministry of Agriculture, then joined the "Water Planning for Israel" (TAHAL) firm, which had just been established until my retirement on the first of April 1987. For more than twenty years I held the position of head of the Drainage and Development Department of that firm that employed up to 30 Engineers and Technicians. The team dealt with regulating rivers in order to prevent floods, agricultural drainage and with constructing about 200 reservoirs for collecting floodwater and purified sewage for irrigation for agricultural settlements in all the country from the Golan Heights up to Eilath.

The department also advised and planned projects for many companies as Mekoroth, The Jewish Agency, Dead Sea Works, The Israeli Electricity Company and more.

In the two photos presented in the following page I appear at the party arranged by TAHAL for employees of the company who have been with it for 25 years. In one of the photos I am getting a present from the director of the firm Eng. Aharon Wiener and in the second- I congratulate the firm on behalf of the Haifa branch.

At the party arranged by TAHAL for employees of the company who have been with it for 25 years.

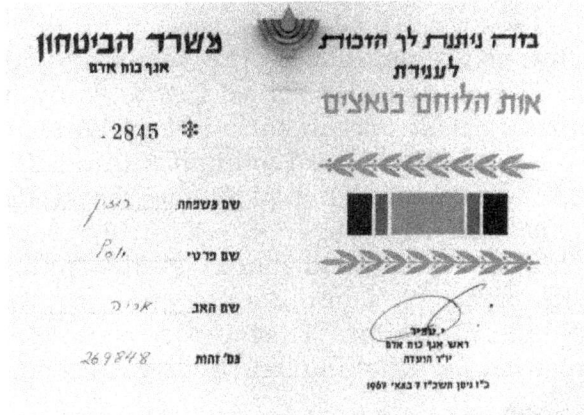

"The Medal as a fighter against the Nazis" granted by the Israeli Defense Ministry

Certificate of discharge from the army

The decorations for participation in the 4 wars

The Family

Amikam (Ami for short) finished his studies at the Technion with a M.Sc. degree in Electronic Engineering. He served in the Army in the Engineering Combat Unit and took part in the Six Day War. He married Irith (nee Oher), also a graduate of the Technion with a B.Sc. degree in Biochemistry. Later she received her M.Sc. degree at the Witwatersrand University in Johannesburg (S.A.). They have a daughter Sharon (born 1972) and a son Gil (born 1975). Sharon studied Accounting at UCLA and Gil Computer Sciences at the California State University in Fullerton. They have completed their studies and are successfully working in their vocations.

In March 2008, Sharon married Aviv Meraro, a graduate in Computer Science of Haifa University. Their beautiful wedding took place in Haifa. In 2010 Sharon gave birth to her daughter Carmel and gave birth in 2013 to her daughter Morielle.

Eliyah was born in 1959 in Haifa. She is an educational psychologist with a M.A. degree from Haifa University. She has two daughters, Lior (born 1995) from her marriage to Tsevi Toren and Inbar (born1988), from her previous marriage to Amir Veg. Inbar is a lovely and very sociable girl, a graduate "with distinction" from the Nahalal High School, now studying at the University of Be'er Sheva Economics and Psychology.

She served in the Army in the Intelligence Unit and is still in the Reserves.

Lior is a nice and a clever girl, a good student in 10th grade at the Nahalal High School. She is also an instructor in the youth organization "The working and studying youth."

Irith   Ami

Sharon   2001   Gil

Inbar and Lior, May 2001

Inbar and Lior 2009

Marches (Tseadoth)

In the seventies of the 20th century we participated in twenty marches the majority of which were organized by 'HaPoel" sports organization. We walked 10 km, 14 km and once as many as 20 km. Among the most popular marches was the Gilboa March which took place at the time when the Gilboa Iris flowers were in full bloom, and we participated in six of these marches. The second most popular march was the Yechiam March, and we completed these five times over the years. The following one was the Menashe Forests March (four times), followed by the Kinereth, Galil and other marches. At the end of every march we got a medal and a certificate. (see photo below).

צעדת הגליל-מבצר נמרוד
1973

The Galil March-Nimrod Castle 1973

Lebanon Border March 1972
From left: Elia, Ada Galin, Asher Galin, Josef and Peninah

Peninah, Tsevika, Eliyah and Josef in August 1994

Eliyah and Tsevika

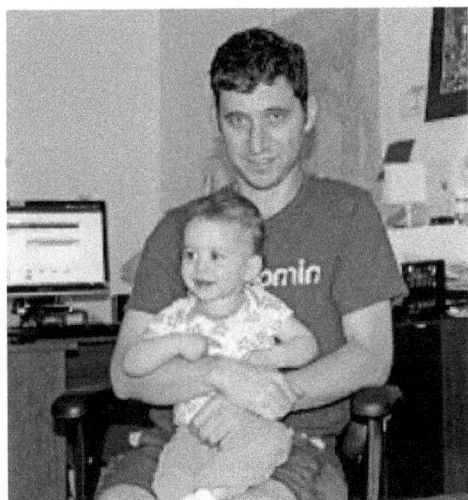

Aviv, Sharon, Carmel, 2011

Eliyah, Inbar, Lior

Liman Grove Meeting 1975

From left: Peninah, Dinah Steinberg, Esther Rubin, Yona Rokhman, Hanah Rokhman, Nehemyah Endlin's wife

Meetings of the Partisans and Underground members

For more than forty years the Partisans and the Underground members of the Kovno ghetto living in Israel held an annual meeting. The meetings took place mostly in Kibbutzim where members of our group were residing, such as Tel Yits'hak, Reshafim, Kefar Masarik, Eilon, Givath Brener, Yagur, Lehavoth Habashan or in locations like Ako, the Hadera Forest, Moshav Kidron, the Liman Grove and more. I together with Peninah and Ami and later with Eliyah, took part in almost all meetings. They were joyful events. (see pictures).

During one of the earlier meetings it was decided to compile a book on the Underground and the Partisans of the Kovno ghetto. The late Tsevi Brown and Dov Levin (later both Professors at the Hebrew University in Jerusalem) were assigned to lead the project. In 1962 the book "The Story of an Underground" was published in Hebrew (422 pages) followed by an English summary (17 pages) by Yad Vashem in Jerusalem.

Tel Yits'hak Meeting 1958

From left: Rachel Rozentsvaig-Levin,......,Josef Smali, Rachel Zagai-Rozner, Hayim Galin, ..., Malka Smali, I, Peninah, Shabtai Pogir, Devorah Yits'haki, Michael Yits'haki, Hinda Katshenovski, Baruch Gofer.

Sitting: Peninah Gofer, Dinah Galin, Tsipi Gofer, Ami,.......

Camping

During these years we would go camping almost every summer. We would load all the camping equipment we owned on the rooftop and in the trunk of the car. In the car Peninah, the initiator of the camping idea, and in most cases Elia and Nivah would join in, and off we would go to one of the camping sites. We went to Neve Yam, Ein Gev, Kefar Hitim, Neve Zohar etc. In most cases our friends Grisha, Beraha and Miri Shufman and Dov and Bilhah Levin would join us as well (see photo).

Neve Zohar 1978

Camping at Neve Zohar with Dov and Bilha Levin

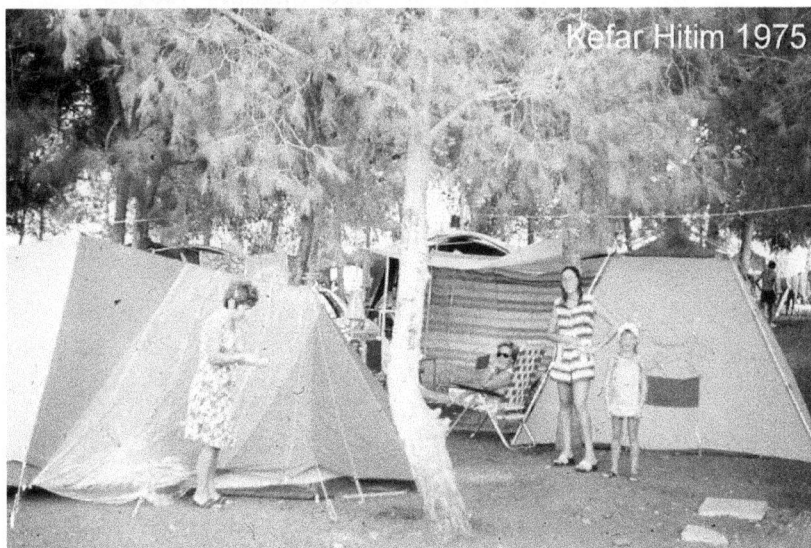

Kefar Hitim 1975

Camping at Kefar Hitim with the Shufman family
From left: Berahah, Peninah, Eliah, Miri

Abroad

In 1981 we traveled abroad for the first time and from then until 1994 we visited the USA six times, Canada twice, England twice, France twice, Scotland, Hawaii, Netherlands, Switzerland, Italy, Austria, Hungary, Croatia, Slovenia. In 1994 we went to the Czech Republic and Poland where we visited the terrible Death Camps, historical sites and also Wloclawek, Peninah's home town. This was our last major trip. (see photo).

Empire State Building 1981

On the top of the Empire State Building 1981

1989

With Josef's cousin Sylvia Rosin-Gendel and her family
in a restaurant in Dallas
From left: Weitz, Sylvia, Loyce Weitz, her son Lane, his wife,
Josef and, Peninah

Commemoration Works

After retiring I began to work on the commemoration of Lithuania's Jewish communities which were annihilated during the Holocaust. At first I wrote a Yizkor book about my home town Kibart (Kybartai-October 1988) which I later translated and can be found on line at JewishGen.org in the KehilaLinks Project. http://kehilalinks.jewishgen.org/kibart/Kibart.html. On the occasion of the publication of this book into Hebrew, a party was arranged at the club of the "Association of Lithuanian Jewry" in Tel Aviv. (see picture)

Delivering a speech at the party

My ex-teacher A.Varshavsky (Bar-Shavit) speaking at the party
(see Postscript)
On the right, the late Zisel Kovensky, the chairman of "The Association of former Kibart Jews in Israel", celebrating his 80th birthday.

In October 1989 I published my "Memoirs." Its third edition I translated into English in 1994, which was then distributed to my close and distant relatives in USA. This is now the updated edition revised in July 2011.

Over a period of about seven years I wrote the entries (about 80%) for the "Encyclopedia of the Jewish Communities in Lithuania" (Pinkas HaKehilot-Lita), published by Yad Vashem in 1996. The editor, my friend Professor Dov Levin, guided my work. I was the Assistant Editor of this extensive book (748 pages).

I helped my wife Peninah publish her memoirs "Pirkei Khayim" in 1996 and in 1997 I translated it into English, naming it "Chapters in my Life." In 2006 Peninah's book "Flight to Survival," edited by our friend Nancy Lefkowitz, was published by JewishGen. Inc. in USA. (185 pages in hard cover) (see photo).

I also printed and advised my childhood friend the late David Shadkhanovitz to publish his biography "Memoirs from the Great

Journey" (1996). I did the same with the Memoirs of my friend Nisan Avizohar-Klorman, whose book was published in 1997.

During the 1990's I wrote 31 articles on the Jewish communities of Lithuania in English, which were posted online on JewishGen, the Kehilalinks section.

Up until today I receive assessment letters and questions from descendants of Lithanian Jews from all over the world.

I am grateful to my friends Sarah and Mordechai Kopfstein of Haifa, who edited most of my English writings and translations, as well as to my second cousin Fania-Hilelson-Jivotovsky from Montreal, Canada, who also edited a number of them.

Thanks to the encouragement and help of my good friend Joel Alpert from near Boston, Massachusetts, USA (my great-grandmother, Elka Rosin, a widow, married Joel's great-great grandfather, Hillel Naividel, a widower in Yurburg, Lithuania) during the years 2005-2009 three books I have written on the history of 102 Jewish communities in Lithuania were published:

1. Preserving Our Litvak Heritage, 31 communities including the Yizkor Book on Kybartai, published by JewishGen, Inc. 2005, 705 pages

2. Preserving Our Litvak Heritage, Vol. II, 21 communities, published by JewishGen, Inc. 2007, 294 pages

3. Protecting Our Litvak Heritage, 50 communities, published by the Friends of the Jewish Yurburg Cemetery, Inc. 2009, 438 pages. (see photos of this book as a sample)

Flight to Survival

Włocławek – Warszawa
Częstochowa...Eretz Yisrael

1939-1945

A personal narrative

Peninah Cypkewicz-Rosin

Published by JewishGen, Inc.
An affiliate of the
Museum of Jewish Heritage - A Living Memorial to the Holocaust

About the author . . .

Peninah (Pola) Cypkewicz was only seventeen years old when the German army entered Włocławek, her home town, on September 14, 1939.

As a result of their treatment by the Nazis and the terror felt by the Jews in the town, her family unit disintegrated. Her father and brother managed to escape to Russia. Peninah and her mother embarked on the dangerous trip to her aunt's home in Warsaw.

For almost five and a half years under Nazi rule, Peninah survived with a combination of initiative and much luck. She traveled from Warsaw to the HaShomer HaTzair farm in Zbarki. From there she went to a kibbutz in Częstochowa, managing to avoid the ongoing liquidations of the town's ghettos and underground, and finally working for almost a year and a half for the Germans at the Hasag munitions factory.

After the liberation from Nazi rule in January 1945, Peninah began a seven month journey to Eretz Yisrael organized by the Briha (escape in Hebrew). She traveled through Poland, Slovakia, Hungary, and Rumania (where she met and married Josef Rosin). Together, they went on to Hungary and Austria, finally arriving in Italy. Once there, she and Josef were crowded into a small fishing vessel with 175 others. After a harrowing seven days at sea and running the British blockade, they arrived in Eretz Yisrael as illegal immigrants. The date was October 25, 1945 six years after the beginning of the Nazi impact on her life.

Peninah's story is one of tremendous personal courage in the face of despair persistence in her struggle to survive, and the ultimate reward – a happy family life with her husband, their two children and four grandchildren in Israel.

This book is a compelling read, a story you will not soon forget.

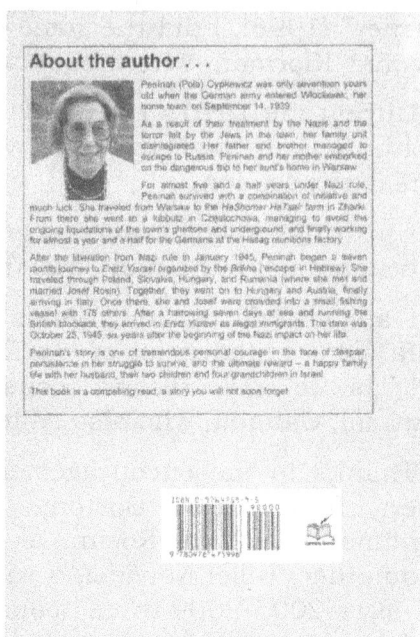

Peninah's Book

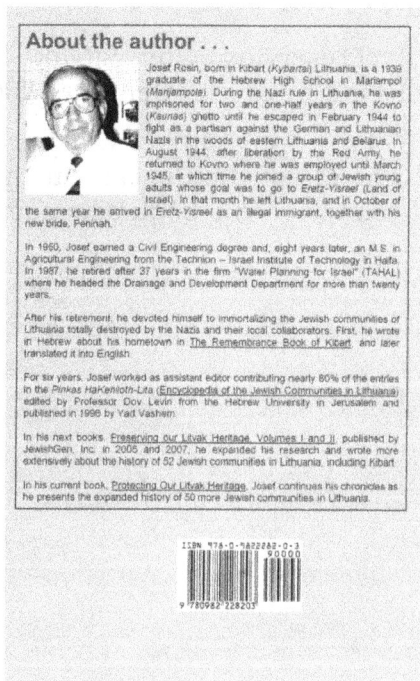

Protecting Our Litvak Heritage

A History of 50 Jewish Communities in Lithuania

by

Josef Rosin

Introduction by Professor Dov Levin

Joel Alpert and Sue Levy, Editors

Published by The Friends of the Yurburg Jewish Cemetery, Inc.
Coral Gables, Florida

About the author . . .

Josef Rosin, born in Kibart (Kybartai) Lithuania, is a 1939 graduate of the Hebrew High School in Mariampol (Marijampole). During the Nazi rule in Lithuania, he was imprisoned for two and one-half years in the Kovno (Kaunas) ghetto until he escaped in February 1944 to fight as a partisan against the German and Lithuanian Nazis in the woods of eastern Lithuania and Belarus. In August 1944, after liberation by the Red Army, he returned to Kovno where he was employed until March 1945, at which time he joined a group of Jewish young adults whose goal was to go to Eretz-Yisrael (Land of Israel). In that month he left Lithuania, and in October of the same year he arrived in Eretz-Yisrael as an illegal immigrant, together with his new bride, Peninah.

In 1960, Josef earned a Civil Engineering degree and, eight years later, an M.S. in Agricultural Engineering from the Technion – Israel Institute of Technology in Haifa. In 1997, he retired after 37 years in the firm "Water Planning for Israel" (TAHAL) where he headed the Drainage and Development Department for more than twenty years.

After his retirement, he devoted himself to immortalizing the Jewish communities of Lithuania totally destroyed by the Nazis and their local collaborators. First, he wrote in Hebrew about his hometown in The Remembrance Book of Kibart, and later translated it into English.

For six years, Josef worked as assistant editor contributing nearly 80% of the entries in the Pinkas HaKehiloth-Lita (Encyclopedia of the Jewish Communities in Lithuania) edited by Professor Dov Levin from the Hebrew University in Jerusalem and published in 1996 by Yad Vashem.

In his next books, Preserving our Litvak Heritage, Volumes I and II, published by JewishGen, Inc. in 2005 and 2007, he expanded his research and wrote more extensively about the history of 52 Jewish communities in Lithuania, including Kibart.

In his current book, Protecting Our Litvak Heritage, Josef continues his chronicles as he presents the expanded history of 50 more Jewish communities in Lithuania.

Josef's Book (The third of the three)

In October 1996, during the annual memorial assembly for Lithuanian Jewry, I was invited to light a candle in memory of the partisans and underground members of the Kovno Ghetto.

Josef Rosin ighting a candle on behalf of the Partisans and Underground Members of the Kovno Ghetto at the Annual Remembrance Assembly of Lithuanian Jewry, Tel-Aviv 1996

Cousin Joel Alpert and his wife Nancy Lefkovitz

Anniversary Celebrations

In June 1995 Peninah and I celebrated our Golden Wedding Anniversary at the "Shulamith" Hotel in Haifa with 70 invited friends. Ami and Irith arrived for this occasion from the USA and Ami chaired this pleasant evening, which consisted of dinner and speeches recalling shared memories for those who were present on this occasion.

In May 2005 we celebrated our 60th annivesary at a restaurant in Haifa together with our family. We belatedly celebrated our 65th anniversary in May 2011 with close family at our home.

At our"Golden Wedding", June 1995
Sitting from left: Eliyah, Inbar, Irith, Ami, I, Rivkah Panush-Shemesh
Standing: Peninah, Khanah

Our 60 anniversary celebration 2005
Top row from left: Josef, Eliya, Hana, Ami, Naor,
Bottom row: Penina, Lior, Zosha, Irith, Nivah, Vered, Yits'hak, Tsevika

Shemuel and his Family

Penina's brother Shemuel, who was in the USSR during WWII, arrived in Israel in 1948. Here he married Khana (nee Weiss) and raised two children, Niva and Naor. Both received academic educations, married and each of them has three daughters. Naor has another little girl from his second marriage.

For many years he worked in the Israeli Shipyards. He progressed steadily at work, learned technical drawing and became a foreman. In 1969 he was sent to the "Lursen" shipyards in Germany for half a year in order to qualify in building motor gun boats for the Navy. On his return he was appointed section boss (No. 14). He did well at work and in 1981 was awarded "The Distinguished Worker" citation on behalf of "The Israel General Workers Organization."

Over the years we have had very close connections with him and his family.

To my regret he passed away after a difficult illness in 1992 at the age of 69. More recently, Khana passed away at the age of 84.

At the commemoration of Shemuel beside its tombstone in 2008
From left: Naor, Nivah, Oriyan (Naor's daughter), Elia, Josef, Peninah, Khana

Bibliography (In Hebrew)

Gar Josef - The Destruction of the Jewish Kovno (in Yiddish), München, 1948.

Belsky Tuviyah and Zusia - Jews of the Woods. Sifriyat Poalim, Tel Aviv, 1946.

Rosin Josef - From the Kovno Ghetto to the Woods, Mishmar, Tel Aviv, 15.11.1946.

Garfunkel L.-The Destruction of Kovno's Jewry, Yad Vashem, Jerusalem, 1959.

Brown A. Zvie & Levin Dov - The Story of an Underground, Yad Vashem, Jerusalem, 1962.

Endlin Nekhemiyah - In the Ways of Guerrilla Fight, Moreshet, Tel Aviv, 1983

The Jewish Partisans Tom 1 Sifriyat Poalim, Tel Aviv, 1958.

Rosin Josef - Kybartai (Lithuania), Haifa, October 1988

Faitelson Alex (Alter)-The Time of Storms and Fights Y.L.Peretz Publishing House, Tel Aviv 1994

Rosin-Cypkewitz Peninah-Chapters in my Life, Haifa 1996

Tec Nechama-Defiance. The Bielsky Partisans (English), Oxford University Press, 1993

YIVO New York, Kibart Jewish Community-Archives

MAJOR EVENTS IN THE WORLD DURING THE YEARS OF MY MEMOIRS

30.1.1933   Hitler became Chancellor (Prime Minister) of Germany.

1.4.1933   The boycott of Jewish shops, doctors, lawyers started in Germany.   The free world reacted with a boycott of German merchandise.

9.1934   The ship "Vilos" made its second sailing from Europe to Eretz Yisrael with 360 illegal immigrants on board. This was the beginning of "Illegal Aliya" which, over the years, brought about 120,000 "Olim" (immigrants to Israel) to Eretz Yisrael, until the establishment of the State of Israel on 14.5.1948.

15.9.1935   "The Law to protect German Blood and Honor" was enacted and as a result the Jews in Germany were banned from all aspects of life. The first Ghettos were established.

19.4.1936   The so called "Arab Uprising" in Eretz Yisrael began, which lasted until the Second World War and resulted in hundreds of Jewish victims.

18.7.1936   The beginning of the Spanish civil war, with the fascist General Franco ruling"

9.11.1938   "Crystal Night" in Germany, when hundreds of synagogues were burned down and thousands of Jews sent to concentration camps.

1.9.1939   The German Army invaded Poland and conquered this country within a few weeks. Plotting against the Jews in Poland began.

23.11.1939   The wearing of the "Yellow Patch", being a mark of a Jew, became obligatory in occupied Poland.

10.5.1940   The German Army invaded Holland, Belgium and Luxembourg.

14.6.1940   The Germans entered Paris without any resistance.

15.6.1940   The Red Army occupied Lithuania and turned it into a Soviet Republic.

22.6.1940   France and Germany signed an armistice agreement, according to which
3/5 of France was in German hands.

20.12.1940   1584 illegal immigrants were sent by the Mandatory Government in Eretz Yisrael to the Island of Mauritius in the Indian Ocean.

<u>27.4.1940</u>   Greece capitulated to Germany.

<u>29.5.1941</u>   The army of the German General Rommel reached the border of Egypt and threatened the Jewish community in Eretz Yisrael.

<u>22.6.1941</u>   The start of the German Army's invasion of the Soviet Union.

<u>8.7.1941</u>   The "Yellow Patch" becomes obligatory for all Jews in the Baltic States (including Lithuania).

<u>6.12.1941</u>   Hundreds of thousands of Jews were murdered in the occupied territories by the Germans.

<u>7.12/1941</u>   Japanese airplanes bombed the American Naval Base in Pearl Harbor in Hawaii causing great damage. Japan joined Germany as an ally in the war.

<u>20.1.1942</u>   The convention of Nazi leaders in Wannsee (near Berlin), where the "Final Solution" decision was taken, i.e. the extermination of all 11 million Jews in Europe.

<u>9.5.1942</u>   The World Zionist Organization proclaimed its plan for the establishment of a Jewish State in Eretz Yisrael.

<u>Summer 1942</u>. The "Death Camps" in Poland (Treblinka, Maidanek, Auschwitz etc.) functioned to full capacity and Jews from all over Europe were transported to them.

<u>4.11.1942</u> The complete victory of the British eighth Army over the Germans in North Africa eliminated the threat to Eretz Yisrael.

<u>31.1.1943</u> The turning point in the war. 330,000 German soldiers were killed in Stalingrad and hundred thousands more were captured, together with their Generals.

<u>19.4.1943</u> The Jewish Underground in the Warsaw Ghetto started its uprising. The battle lasted until 8.5.1943, when the last bunker fell and with it the leader of the uprising, Mordechai Anilevitz. More than 1,000 Germans were killed in this battle.

<u>During 1943</u>. The murder of the Jews in Poland and Russia continued.

<u>24.2.1944</u> The start of the great attack of the Red Army in Bielorussia.

<u>5.3.1944</u> Attacks on three fronts in the Ukrainian Republic by the Red Army.

<u>6.6.1944</u> The Allied invasion of occupied France.

13.7.1944.   Vilna liberated by the Red Army.

19.9.1944   The establishment of the Jewish Brigade in the British Army. (Dismantled 10.7.1946)

20.7.1944   An attempt to kill Hitler by high officers of the German Army (Wehrmacht) failed. Hundreds of officers were executed.

26.1.1945   The Auschwitz "Death Camp" was freed by the Red Army.

29.4.1945   The American Army freed 82,000 prisoners from Dachau, the worst concentration camp in Germany.

30.4.1945   Hitler committed suicide by swallowing poison in his bunker in Berlin. The Red Army hoisted its flag on the Reichstag (Parliament) in Berlin.

7.5.1945   The end of the war. Germany surrenders unconditionally to the allies. About 30 million people, soldiers and civilians, were killed in the war, amongst them six million Jews.

6.8.1945   An atomic bomb was dropped by the American Air Force on the Japanese city of Hiroshima. About 100,000 people were killed.

9.8.1945   Another atomic bomb was dropped on the Japanese city of Nagasaki. 18,000 buildings were totally ruined and 40,000 people killed.

14.8.1945   Japan capitulated and the Second World War came to its end. Only five States in the world kept their neutrality.

 25.9.1945   The first convention of Jewish survivors of the camps in Germany was opened in the concentration camp of Bergen-Belsen, with 200 delegates attending. The resolution of that convention called for the gates of Eretz Yisrael to be opened to unlimited "Aliya".

20.11.1945 In Nuremberg the trials of 24 German war criminals opened before an international military court.

14.12.1945   11 of the commanders of Bergen-Belsen and Auschwitz were hanged by the British.

Appendices

Mazampol den 17.10.15.
Lieber Bruder!
Wer hat in seinem Leben
so viel Freude gehabt
wie wir, als wir
vor unseren Augen
deine Handschrift
ersehen haben? Jetzt
hoffentlich wird unser
Korrespondenz veröffert
werden. Schreib, lieber
Bruder-l vorläufig
auf die Adresse des
Bruders, an ihn kommt
schneller an. Ich bin
froh dass Du so fröhlich

und munter bist
Schreib, wie viel Du
verdienst hast Du
genug für deinen Geb-
rauch? Mir machte
es viel Verdruss, dass
Du so beunruhigt
bist über den Eltern,
dafür werden sie
schon dies-mal einen
Gruss aufschreiben.
Uns geht's im Alge-
meinen nichts schlecht
aber doch wäre schon
Zeit gewesen, der Krieg
sollte schon zu Ende

Table 4

nehmen. ich habe
viel sehr viel Dir
zu erzählen, wollen
wir aber hoffen, dass es
wieder uns Gutes anfref-
fen wird, dass wir
noch mals wieder
zusammen sein werden.
Mit den herzlichsten
Grüssen und Küssen
von deiner benkende
Schwester,
M. Leibowitz
Es grüsst herzlich
Deine Mutter

Ich grüsse dir in Würde
alles gutes wie es fodert
Dein
P.S. Wenn Du eine
Antwort schreibst
schreibe doch, bitte
wie es allen Mazam-
poler geht? hauptsäch-
lich von Rahel Grodisch
et Familie.
Es grüsst Dich herzlich
Deine Schwester
Minna

Table 4a

Table 4a

Table 5

Table 7

Table 7

Table 8

קויגס, 27 XI.32

אחי היקר !

[handwritten Hebrew letter]

The 5 pages of 11 are the letter I wrote to my uncle Baruch on 1,9.1944.
Table 11

Table 11 a

Table 11 b

Table 11 c

Table 11 d

INDEX

Rozner, 172
Rubin, 171
Rubinshtein, 146
Rudman, 75

S

Saalkind, 28
Saharovitz, 57
Sandovski, 153
Seinensky, 2
Serban, 50
Shadkhanovitz, 2, 9, 18, 25, 32, 56, 60, 63, 70, 176
Shapira, 85, 86, 88, 89, 133
Shatenstein, 34
Shefer, 103, 105, 124, 135, 146, 149, 161
Sheinzon, 61
Shemesh, 161, 180
Sherman, 123
Shmulevitz, 144, 146, 149, 156
Shnucal, 82, 83, 86, 87
Shnukal, 97
Shtern, 57, 123
Shtrom, 104, 108, 123
Shub, 106, 161
Shufman, 173
Simon, 13, 91, 92, 101
Simonov, 110
Smali, 172
Smilg, 65
Steinberg, 171
Stern, 34, 59
Sukenik, 103, 133
Surkis, 153, 160

T

Tager, 57
Telser, 12
Telshitz, 12, 25, 54
Teper, 123, 134
Toren, 143, 144, 164
Tratsevitsky, 148, 149
Tratsevitzky, 144
Trushin, 111, 112
Tur Zion, 103
Turkenitz, 23

V

Vald, 32, 33, 72, 73, 76, 128
Varshavsky, 55, 58, 61, 176
Veg, 164
Vidokle, 146
Vidomliansky, 57
Vilensky, 3, 58
Vitenshtein, 65
Vitkauskas, 78
Vittenberg, 64
Vizhansky, 30, 34, 57
Vizhanzky, 34
Volchansky, 57
Voskoboinik, 104

W

Weiss, 181
Weitz, 44, 50, 174
Wiener, 162

Y

Yaffe, 61
Yaskulka, 156
Yelin, 100, 102, 107
Yeshmanta, 65
Yits'haki, 172
Yofe, 57
Yukhnikov, 123

Z

Zagai, 133, 142, 160, 172
Zaharik, 57
Zaitsev, 123
Zapolsky, 48
Zhukov, 126, 127
Zilber, 123
Zilberfarb, 156
Zilbersky, 58
Ziman, 100, 110
Zinger, 146
Zohar, 142, 173
Zorin, 115, 116, 120, 121, 122, 123, 124, 125
Zupovitz, 92, 96, 103

www.ingramcontent.com/pod-product-compliance
Lightning Source LLC
Chambersburg PA
CBHW050359110426
42812CB00006BA/1743